Following Joey Home

Following Joey Home

Meg Woodson

**ZONDERVAN
PUBLISHING HOUSE** OF THE ZONDERVAN CORPORATION
GRAND RAPIDS, MICHIGAN 49506

FOLLOWING JOEY HOME

© 1978 by Meg Woodson

This printing 1980

Library of Congress Cataloging in Publication Data

Woodson, Meg.
   Following Joey home.

   1. Cystic fibrosis—Biography.   2.   Terminally
ill children—Biography.   3.   Woodson, Joey.
4.   Consolation.   I.   Title.
RJ456.C9W65   618.9'23'7   [B]   77-29009

ISBN 0-310-34861-7

Printed in the United States of America

To Joey — My Special *Joye*

Introduction

It is impossible to write a book about Joey Woodson without including an explanation of cystic fibrosis. C.F. is a difficult disease to explain, however, because it affects the sweat glands and mucus-producing glands, glands which exist throughout the body and the malfunction of which affects the body in a variety of ways.

C.F. patients perspire profusely, and their sweat has a high salt content. They are uncomfortable in hot weather. Their pancreatic glands produce a thick, sticky mucus which interferes with digestion. C.F. patients take enzymes with every meal to aid in the absorption of food, but they are still generally small and thin.

It is the glands in the lungs that are the real culprits, however, for here the viscous mucus secreted clogs the airways, creating breathing difficulties, high susceptibility to infection, and progressive lung damage.

Afflicted children and young adults sleep in mist tents at night and breathe aerosols two to four times every day to help thin the mucus. Parents or friends pound and vibrate the lungs to enable the mucus to be coughed up, much as you pound and shake a catsup bottle to encourage the catsup to run out.

Cystic fibrosis is a distant reality to most Americans, but one out of every two thousand babies is born with this disease. To these victims and to their families it is as close as breathing, and as crucial.

This book is based on a diary I kept during Joey's last hospitalization. In every way that counts it is a true story.

Acknowledgments

Thank you, members of the Cuyahoga County Writers Workshop, for working through this book with me. I am equally grateful for your sweat and your tears. Thank you especially, Janet Smith and Joanne Denko and Sue Balika, for your special support; and thank you, Jan, for the book's title. Thank you, too, Dina Donohue and Jean Maddern Pitrone, for your wise, sacrificial guidance. Without the warm, professional help all of you gave me, this book could not have been written.

And thank you, members of the Church in the Woods of Parma Heights, Ohio, for living through the events of this book with me. You were there when I needed you, and I will never forget you. Thank you, too, for releasing me from the role of traditional minister's wife. Without the freedom you gave me, this book could not have been written.

And thank you, husband, for keeping my spirits high; and thank you, teen-age daughter, for keeping them humble. Thank you both for always being there—for bearing the brunt of my frustration when the writing went poorly, and for crawling into unmade beds when the writing went well. Without the love you gave me, this book could not have been written.

I bought a spiral notebook today. I felt inspired to buy it, as I feel inspired now to sit here scribbling in it, recording the events and emotions of the past week. Time hangs heavy in this room. There's not enough to do to fill the hours. Yet in another way time is careening by with out-of-control speed. I want to slow the minutes, hold on to every second. Perhaps that's why I am compelled to capture them here on paper. I want it to be a part of me forever, the way things are today, the way things were on what I think of as that first day, that

First Friday

The house was a castle that first Friday night—a castle waiting for its king.

The king wasn't scheduled to arrive till the next morning, and the announcement of his imminent coming caused a good bit of scurrying about.

"Joey doesn't care what the house looks like, mother," Peggie, the king's sister, objected.

"Well, I care," I said. No better way could I prepare for my sovereign, twelve-year-old though he be, than by straightening things up.

When before had so many headlights shone through our front windows? Would Joey's coach never arrive?

"I bet you never made this much fuss over me," Peg protested. Peggie, like her brother, had cystic fibrosis and was used to her own homecomings from the hospital.

I understood her lack of understanding, for she was just two years older than Joey, and Joe and I had been careful to shelter her from the fear that had howled inside us for weeks—the fear that Joey might never come home.

"You should talk," I told her, squeezing her playfully. "You're as excited as I am."

"I'm gonna get Teddy and Ms. Mildred," she said. "We can't have a family reunion without them." And, teen-ager that she was, she ran upstairs to get the bedraggled tan bear and his purple and white spouse, stuffed animals that for years had served as substitutes for the live pets the children could not have.

Just then the royal chariot pulled in the drive. And seconds later a small, unbelievably skinny boy stood in the front hall, glasses halfway down his nose, T-shirt all the way out of his jeans, his head crowned only by an eight-week growth of straight brown hair. One borrowed television set; one pillow-case full of dirty clothes; two suitcases bulging with a jumble of models, books, puzzles, and get-well cards; and Big Joe, father and minister, composed his train.

"We're late because Joey wouldn't leave till he finished the plaque he was working on," Joe said. "We had to wait for the paint to dry."

Proudly Joey shoved into my hands the piece of plaster of Paris he'd been cradling under one arm, and I looked, eyes swimming, at the swirl of red roses and the words *God Bless Our Home* painstakingly patched in several shades of blue.

Surely our home was blessed.

And then Joey handed me the grocery bag he'd been clutching in his other hand, motioning me down so he could talk in my ear. "The nurse gave me a bag so daddy wouldn't see the Tarzan model," he whispered, referring to the Father's Day surprise we had planned for Joe in honor of his famous lusty jungle yell.

I took advantage of Joey's nearness to give him a big hug, and he threw his arms around my neck and hung tight, being a ruler of exceptional warmth and affection. How good he felt. Oh, how good that whole lean, loose, loving bundle of boy felt.

"Welcome home, Joey," I said.

"Teddy and Ms. Mildred are glad to see you," Peg added, winking at Joe and me. She bobbed Teddy's head at Joey with big-sister indulgence.

"I have to go to the bathroom," the king said, and we all escorted him to the downstairs bath. It was the first of many trips to the throne room that night, but we knew that while Joey did have a kidney problem, it was clearing up.

"I'm hungry. How about some Grape Nuts?" the king asked, and we rushed to do his bidding, I pouring the cereal and Peg the milk.

"Don't expect this kind of service all the time," she warned.

Three bowls of Grape Nuts and five cups of milk his majesty consumed before he pushed back from the table and proceeded on an inspection tour of the house, wandering about patting things happily.

"It sure is good to be home," he said.

"It sure is good to have you home," we agreed.

How tired he seemed. But then he'd had the measles, a disastrous disease for a child with cystic fibrosis, and all those weeks of secondary infection in the hospital had followed.

"If you want to start your 3,000-piece puzzle tomorrow, I'll be your sorter," I said.

"I'll sort too," Joe injected.

Not if I can help it, I thought belligerently. You can work with him on his God and Country Award or play chess with him or help him with his wolf-man model, but everybody knows I'm his official puzzle sorter.

"I think I wanna go to bed," the king said.

We looked at him in amazement and with no little concern at the slowness with which he climbed the stairs. But when he got to his room, his energy returned.

"Hey! New curtains," he cried, pointing to the red and blue drapes.

"Do you like them?" I asked. "And, look, I finally got the Snoopy sheets on your bed, and I washed your quilt just so it'd be nice and soft."

Joey patted the Snoopy sheets and the red and blue quilt. "Yeah, yeah," he said contentedly. "My very own bed. And my books," he added, pointing to the shelves crammed with the most precious of his possessions. "It sure is good to see my books again. And my skull. Is my money still in my skull?"

"I'm sure it is, Joey. Nobody touches that hideous thing but you."

"Why do you think I keep my money in it?" Joey grinned at me sinisterly.

He got ready for bed then, and I tucked him in, getting him the additional cup of milk he requested.

"What's with all this milk?" I asked. "I've always had to beg to get any down you."

"That hospital milk was awful," he replied. "This is my kind of milk."

"How about chicken for dinner tomorrow with blueberry muffins?"

"Yeah, yeah," he said, and smacking his lips puppy-dog style, he patted me on the head.

And then Joe and Peggie came in, and the four of us held hands while Joe prayed. "Thank You, Father, that our son is back with us. Thank You for the doctors and nurses in the hospital and all they did for him. Help us take good care of him now. And help him always to know how much he means to us. In Jesus' name. Amen."

We put down his mist tent and left him then. "We're a family again," Joe said. "We're complete."

In some principalities of ancient days a special flag flew over the palace when the king was in residence. Well, a flag was flying high in our hearts that night, for our Joey was home at last.

First Saturday, First Sunday
Early First Monday Morning

Joey had trouble sleeping that first night at home. "I kept having spells when I couldn't get enough air in my lungs," he said the next morning.

I opened the sofa bed in the family room, offering him the Coke that was part of the routine when one of the children was sick and we opened the couch.

"I'd rather have milk," Joey replied.

Delighted, I jumped in the car to get him another half-gallon. Anything to fatten him up.

We didn't do any of the things we planned to do that day. "I'm just too tired," Joey kept saying. "I just wanna rest." And he lay inert on the couch, his new Hardy Boys book unopened at his side. He roused himself only at mealtimes.

Our church had a Father-Son Banquet that night. I felt sorry for Joe going by himself. We'd never had a Father-Son Banquet before, and he had hoped against hope he'd be able to take his son.

But mostly I felt scared. I knew that children with cystic fibrosis maintained fairly normal activity even in advanced stages of lung scarring. They went into the hospital for intravenous antibiotic treatment, but they roamed about having the time of their lives while they were there. Joey should be getting less tired, not more tired.

On Sunday he complained of a couple more spells when he couldn't catch his breath.

"The doctor says your lungs are fairly clear," I told him. "There's no physical reason for you to be having this problem."

"Then why am I having it?"

"Well, you remember what the nurses said. You were in the hospital so long it became a way of life for you. You're probably upset at being away. Just being tense can bring on attacks like this."

Nevertheless, I stayed close all day and that evening, too.

And then in the middle of the night we heard Joey scream, a terrible scream, and we ran to his room. "I can't get any air in my lungs," he cried. "I can't. I can't."

We believed him this time. We watched in unbelief as his whole body gulped convulsively for air. Joe picked him up and carried him into our room, the heat from his slight body burning through Joe's pajamas. How small he looked lying in the middle of our big bed. And then it began again, Joey throwing himself from one end of the bed to the other in spasm-like efforts to breathe.

Never had I been that frightened.

Four A.M. I called Dr. Rathburn.

"Bring him to the emergency room," he said.

Joe hurtled through every red light we hit on that mad trip across a deserted city. "God is so close, isn't He?" he said. Joe was my rock.

A huge young attendant waited for us at the door of the emergency room. "Come with me, big fella," he said kindly and, lifting Joey effortlessly from the back seat, bore him away.

Later the doctor talked to us. "It's not his lungs. It's his heart. When he left the hospital, the size of his heart was normal. Now it's significantly enlarged. Did he have anything unusual to eat or drink while he was home?"

"Well, he must have had a gallon or two of milk."

The doctor gasped. "Milk is loaded with sodium. With his kidneys not functioning fully, his heart couldn't handle —"

"What's going to happen to Joey, doctor?" My voice shook, and Joe put his arm around my shoulders protectingly.

"Joey doesn't have enough lung damage to have brought on heart failure. Not knowing what caused it, I can't predict the result."

"But what do you think? What's your best judgment?"

"It's an ominous development."

We went to the ward where they'd taken Joey and stood by as the nurses put him in an ice pack—injected him with a diuretic—prepared an oxygen tent.

Joey settled down at last, and Joe and I settled down beside him for what remained of the wee hours.

Later that morning the doctor had him moved to a private room. "I want him to rest as much as possible," he said. But I'd been around the hospital long enough to know what being moved to a private room meant.

It was a harmless enough procession we made. Joey was pushed in his bed, nurses and aides following with his bedside table and suitcase and I.V. pole; I brought up the rear, empty-handed, wordless. But I knew what kind of march this was.

A death march.

Later First Monday Morning

Frozen in fear was more than a metaphor that first Monday morning as I sat beside Joey's bed, body stiff, mind numb. I could not move because any motion on my part might start a chain reaction. If I did not move, maybe Joey would continue to lie there unmoving. Unmoving but breathing.

The nurses came and went. Did EKGs repeatedly. Checked the oxygen. I stared at them through sunken eyes. I could not think because I dared not go where my thoughts might lead me.

Dr. Rathburn came in, listened to Joey's chest, and walked silently from the room, as was to become his habit. I followed him silently, as was to become mine.

"What's going to happen to Joey, doctor?" Why did I insist on being told what I resisted believing?

"I'm pessimistic about combinations of diseases."

"How long does he have?"

"I can't predict."

"Will you be able to give us some warning when the time comes?"

He said he thought he would. He said it frustrated him to talk to me, always having to say the same thing. "I don't know. I can't predict."

It frustrated me, too. "Can't you make any kind of prognosis?"

"Well, here's what we have. A child with cystic fibrosis. A child with a second disease, a deficiency of the enzyme alpha one anti-trypsin, a deficiency which even apart from cystic fibrosis leads to chronic lung problems. I never had a patient with both these diseases till your children came along.

"Then you add heart failure to these two, and you have a third disease, a third primary disease, because Joey's heart failure is left-sided. It's not pulmonary heart failure at all. I've never had a C.F. patient who went into left-sided heart failure."

I appreciated Dr. Rathburn's honesty. I couldn't have taken the added strain of wondering if he were hiding something from me.

"Then there's the fever Joey keeps running," Dr. Rathburn went on. "It's not symptomatic of any of his known diseases. I suspect he has a fourth disease we've not yet identified. All I can tell you is that these diseases interact with each other, that the total effect is far more devastating than the effects of the four or five diseases individually."

I weaved back to my chair like an unwieldy ice mass.

"What took ya so long?" Joey mumbled, as was to become his habit every time I left his side.

"I'm sorry, Joey. I was talking to Dr. Rathburn."

"How'm I doin', mom? Why can't I—ya know—breathe?"

"Well, it's not your lungs, Joey. You've developed a problem with your heart. It's good we know what's wrong because now we can do something about it. Dr. Rathburn says he'll explain things to you when you're not feeling so bad."

"Oh," said Joey, satisfied.

I cried then, for the first time. I could bear with my own worry one way or another, but I could not bear to see this normally carefree child of mine worry. Watching him return so effortlessly to childhood—I melted a little.

Yet I did not lean to pat him reassuringly. For my hands were still too cold to touch his still-warm body.

First Monday Afternoon

Joey had to have a bowel movement that first Monday afternoon, and he refused to use the bedpan. I grabbed the first nurse I saw, the one Peggie called the top sergeant.

"Joey has to go to the bathroom, Dot."

"That's okay. He can go."

"But he's scared, and we don't know what to do about the oxygen. Will you help?"

Dot squeezed my arm. "Sure," she said. "I'll help." And, indeed, her bright, bossy chatter did Joey and me both good on our short trek to the bathroom.

"About face! Forward march!" Dot barked, and finally both sagging, lagging soldiers made it back to the bed.

But then Joey's old trouble returned. "I can't get—enough air—in my lungs," he screamed, his body going into those awful twistings again.

Dot dashed across the hall, grabbed an oxygen mask some other child wasn't using at the moment, and slapped it on Joey's face.

They took away Joey's tent after that and left him with a mask. He didn't mind, but it was hard for me to look at him with that ugly contraption covering half his face.

And then he complained of a pain in his chest. "It's a new pain, mama. Oh, mama, it's a bad pain."

I ran for help again. Joey's intern sent for the portable x-ray equipment. "Joey doesn't have a hole in his lungs," the intern reported. "The pain has to be from his heart."

I know all about pain in the heart, I thought, for I couldn't stay frozen with these crises going on, not when Joey needed me poised for action. I was thawing fast, and the hot pain burned grimly.

Your will be done, Father, I prayed. But, please, if it is Your will, don't let Joey die.

And then I had to convince myself he wasn't dying. How could he be dying when such a short time before he had been so full of life? Why, it had only been a couple months before that I had been down in the basement one morning when it was time for Joey to leave for school. Just this once, I'd thought, busy with the wash, he can leave by himself.

But soon he was hollering down the stairs at me, all boisterous indignation. "Hey, what's the matter? Aren't ya gonna— ya know—see me off?"

And I came up gladly to stand by the front door as he rode down the street on his bike, balancing precariously with one arm full of books, lunch box hanging over the handlebars, baseball jacket flying.

When Joey turned to see if I was still looking, he managed to dodge the kiss I threw. It was a regular game we played—if there were no other kids around. I threw a kiss and he dodged. If he was walking, it went on for quite a while. Sometimes when I threw a kiss he put his thumbs on the sides of his head and waggled his fingers at me.

"Disrespectful child," I'd yell. But then I'd put my thumbs on my head and waggle back at him.

Would I ever see him off for school again? Please, God, he means so much to me. He's such a special kid.

Once during his recent hospitalization as we waited for the elevator together, he had pulled me down close. "When I get home," he said, "you and I'll have a nice, long cuddle in the black chair."

We hadn't had the cuddle. Would we ever have the cuddle?

The point was, though, that Joey enjoyed the feel of me as

much as I enjoyed the feel of him. That was one of the things that made him such a joy, the pleasure he took in me. He rarely complained about anything I did or anything I was. Didn't we all need one person in our lives who accepted us exactly as we were?

Nor was it just me Joey liked. An unsquelchably happy child, Joey cuddled up to life. What would I do without Joey by my side looking at everything with shining eyes?

Far from perfect, he drove me wild with his dawdling and his endless teasing. Miss Murdock, his teacher this past year, who had also been Peggie's sixth grade teacher, said our children were at opposite ends of the maturity spectrum —Peggie exceptionally mature and Joey exceptionally immature.

Yet Joey was my son, my only boy-child. Didn't all mothers have a tender something going with their sons that they didn't have going with anyone else? What good times we had together, even shopping for clothes. Never did Joey stand in a dressing room, all fifty-five pounds of him in his jockey shorts, without going into his Atlas act. I'd laugh until I cried.

I was closer to Peggie than I was to Joey. And Joe had his unique place in my heart. But Joey was my special joy. If I lost him, something would be gone from my life that could never be replaced.

I'd always made sure Joey knew how I felt. "You are the joy of my life," I told him again and again.

Once he had seen me crying over something (I didn't often let him see me cry), and he had gone into my study and then come out and thrown a torn-off piece of paper at me. "You are the Joye to my life," he had scribbled.

One of the nicest things about that little note, I remembered now as I looked at the small form in the hospital bed, was the way he had finished it:

> (Siened) your Beloved son
> Joseph Woodson Jr.

He finished most of his notes to me that way, or with slight variations, such as:

(Sind) Your beLoved Joey W.

The atrocious spelling and rambling scrawl were typical of Joey, but where he'd picked up that word *beloved* I could not imagine. Where had he absorbed a word as uncontemporary as beloved? And why had he used it so consistently? Was it just basic to his being, the knowledge that that's what he was?

Oh, God, that is what he is, You know. Please, God, Your will be done, but don't let Joey be taken from me unless it is Your will—not my beloved Joey W.—not my beloved son.

First Monday Night

I sat in the hospital cafeteria and pushed the cheeseburger back and forth on my plate. Joe had made me come down. "You have to take care of yourself," he said. "I'll be right here with Joey. If anything goes wrong, I can get to you in a minute."

So I came. But I could not eat.

Only my mind was hungry. Why? Why was this happening to Joey?

Why had he gotten the measles anyway? We'd traveled 1200 miles to get the children vaccinated when the measles vaccine had first come out. Joey had been six months old at the time. Now doctors knew that some of the early vaccine had not been effective, especially on small babies. Was Joey simply the victim of incomplete medical knowledge?

And why had he been born with cystic fibrosis in the first place? "You have three out of four chances of having a healthy child," our doctor then had said. "The odds are all with you." How we had prayed that God would step in and control the odds. But had He? Or was Joey simply the victim of an unfortunate throw of the dice?

And what about the anti-trypsin deficiency in his blood? That was hereditary, too, but was there some ultimate cause, some force beyond the laws of heredity, at work here? Why so many mixed-up genes in Joe and me?

And why the mysterious fever? And why the unprecedented milk urge? I wanted to know why Joey's heart had failed. I wanted the medical why, but I wanted more mystical explanations, too. Why one young boy with so many things wrong with him?

They weren't rebellious whys I asked. I'd gotten over my anger at God years ago. Had come to love Him with a consuming love. If God wanted my son, God could have my son. But did He want him? They were curious whys I asked. Wouldn't I react one way if all this were happenstance and another if it were a part of some master design?

I nibbled away on my cheeseburger, taking from my purse the paperback by Elton Trueblood I'd been working through for some time—*Confronting Christ*, a daily commentary on the Gospel of Luke. I leafed through the book, not knowing where I'd left off, and stopped at last at one particular page for no particular reason. I think now it would be more accurate to say I was stopped at that page.

I remember nothing of the commentary, but I will always remember the words from the Bible around which it centered, words God spoke from heaven to Jesus two thousand years ago. For God spoke to me through those words: "You are my beloved son."[1]

I will always remember that first Monday night as I sat in the hospital cafeteria with God's presence upon me and those familiar words drilling their way through my skull. "*You* are my beloved son."

Me. God loved me.

The words were not a rational response to any of my questions. Yet I sensed that they were a response, that no better way could God answer my whys than by saying *I love you*.

I might not be able to understand the mind of God, but to some degree I could understand His heart. I hugged myself securely that night as I took my first uncertain steps into the limitless heart of God.

First Tuesday Morning

I slept on Monday night on a cot the nurses set up for me in Joey's room. And Joe arrived early Tuesday morning. The hospital doesn't make provision for two parents to sleep in, and Peg needed one of us at home, so Joe came and went.

He seemed to want to be alone with Joey, so I wandered down to the Parents' Lounge at the end of the hall. At times during Joey's last hospitalization when he hadn't felt like talking, he'd thumped one white-socked foot at me when I left—another of his puppy-dog things.

Today he lay there motionless. I'd always been such a part of his activities I felt I could not bear his stillness.

How many times in days gone by had he dragged me in to admire a half-completed scene on the dining room table? "How'm I doin' on my puzzle, mom? Do you have time to sort for me?"

Or, "How'm I doin' on my model, mom? Look, it's the *Hoonch*back of Notre Dame. Will you buy some black model paint when you go out?"

Or, "How'm I doin' on my book, mom?" finger displaying how much he'd read.

Now if he said anything, it was, "How'm I doin', mom?" And that was all.

Not too well, Joey, I answered in the quiet of the Parents' Lounge.

How much more I loved him now that I was on the verge of

losing him. At least how much more aware I was of my love. I could not lose a child I loved that much.

Oh, God, I need You. Help.

But hadn't He already helped? What was it He'd been telling me the night before? That He loved me, yes. But there had been something specific about His love that I hadn't put my finger on.

And then it came to me. "You are my *beloved son.*" How had I missed it? God was communicating His love for me in the way I could best take it in right now. As much as you love your beloved Joey W., God was saying, that's how much I love you.

Of course, I'd always known God loved me. But His love had been an unreal thing, so different from human love as to have little attraction for me.

If a friend said "I love you," life was enriched. If my mother said "I love you," that was warmth, health, peace. If my earthly father said "I love you," I was strengthened, enlarged. If my husband said "I love you," that, supposedly, was the end of my quest. But if my heavenly Father-Mother-Lover-Friend said "I love you," . . . Ho hum. What else was new?

So it was a big thing, God telling me He loved me in the same manner, the same measure, as I loved Joey. Do you want your beloved son, Meg? Do you want to be with him? Do you want to do things for him? Well, that's how much I want you. That's how much I want to be with you. With all My being I am working for all that's best for you.

First Tuesday Afternoon and Night

It began normally enough, that Tuesday Joe and I have referred to ever since as *that Tuesday*. But about mid-afternoon Joey had trouble breathing again.

"I can't—get enough—air in my lungs," he gasped. "It's like—that night—you brought me back—to the hospital."

And it was like that night, becoming even worse than that nightmare as the pain that accompanied every breath increased. Except this time no flurry of activity whipped about Joey. Everything that could be done for him had already been done.

"If I were ready to give up on Joey, I'd raise his oxygen," Dr. Rathburn told me. "But I haven't quite reached that point."

"I can't let him die unaware that he is dying," I responded in barely audible tones.

"Wait till he brings up the subject," the doctor replied. "He will, you know. Then tell him that some children who have been as sick as he is have died, while others who have been just as sick have recovered."

I waited. I cemented myself to the edge of the bed, panting along with Joey, beside myself with fear that each laborious inhalation would be our last.

"Check the hose," Joey pleaded. "The oxygen's—not coming through."

"It's okay, Joey. It's coming through. See, I can feel it."

"But I can't—get enough air—in my lungs."

Other kids who had been as sick as Joey might have recovered, but I could tell the nurses didn't expect Joey to. They kept giving me the eye to see how I was doing and patting me or hugging me as they passed.

"Tell the doctor—to turn up—the oxygen."

"I've already asked him, Joey. It's up as far as he can turn it."

"I wanna die."

"Oh, Joey, don't say that."

"Uh-h-h—I wanna die." It was developing into a rhythm, louder and louder groans with each breathing in and then the plea for release.

How I wanted to hold him. I couldn't, of course, but I got as close as I could. Laid my face down next to his on the pillow. "The doctor says you may get better, Joey, but he also says you may not. You may go to heaven very soon."

"Good," Joey mumbled.

"Yes, it will be good. You remember what heaven's like, everybody loving everybody else."

"Yeah—yeah—and no more pain."

"I surely will miss you, though, Joey. Nobody will ever take your place. If I'd thought up exactly the kind of son I wanted, he would have been just like you."

Joey's fingers curled around mine. "I don't suppose—you could—put me—out of my misery?"

I couldn't believe that was my Joey speaking. Not with that big-man air. Not asking that old-man question. "No, honey. When you die is up to God." My control amazed me. Joey wanted to be put out of his misery.

"Will you pray—that God—will let—it be soon?"

"Oh, Joey, daddy'd never forgive me if you died before he got here."

"Where is daddy? When is he—coming?"

"Soon, Joey. I finally got hold of him. But God might not want you to die now, Joey. We never know what God's plan is. You may feel great tomorrow."

It wasn't right for him to be determined to die, especially when he was wearing his pajamas with the blue circles, the pajamas he often wore all day long on Saturdays, too consumed with some puzzle or model even to dress. How *delicious* the lithe thickness of him had felt through the washed-out cotton of those pajamas with the little blue circles.

"Uh-h-h—can't we pray—without daddy?

"Uh-h-h—I wanna—be done—with all this."

"Is there anything you'd like me to tell Peggie for you?" I asked softly.

"Tell her—to take—good care—of Teddy." Joey patted my hand and laughed his familiar high, girlish laugh. I will never forget how he sounded in that moment—laughing.

"Would you like Peggie to have any of your things?" I didn't want to put Joey under unnecessary strain, but I knew how much this would mean to Peggie.

"She can have—any of—my books—she wants. My toys—can go to—the garage sale," he said, referring to the yearly sale of their unwanted possessions that he and Peggie put on together. "Or else—to the—Salvation Army. 'Cept Peggie—can have—anything—she wants."

We were quiet after that, save for the sound of Joey's groaning. I will never forget how he sounded in those moments—groaning.

And then at length he spoke again. "Give my money—to the—roof fund. The church—really—needs it."

I saw no reason to tell him the roof fund had been completed months before. There wasn't anything else to say, and while I kept my head on the pillow next to his, I turned my face away, my tears running uncontrollably.

And then Joe flew in, zoomed in on wings of love and fear.

Joey reached out his hand. "Hi, dada," he cried, reverting to the baby name he still used in moments of affection, relief and joy mingling in his voice. "Will you pray—that God—will let me die?"

Joe stood still for one long moment before he took command.

"I'm going to pray for God's will to be done, Joey," he said, and so he did, leading us aloud in prayer. The chairman of our board of deacons had driven Joe over. A big, brawny man, he sat and wept with us. I don't know what his prayer was, but I honored Joey. I prayed that God would let him die.

I thought I'd surrendered Joey to God before. But this night was something else, this never-to-be-forgotten afternoon and night. To believe it was God's will for Joey to die and to pray for His will to be accomplished.

Our deacon left to spread the news of Joey's imminent death throughout the congregation. The young man who had directed C.F. Camp for the five glorious years Joey had attended came down from Inhalation Therapy and replaced Joey's mask with a forked tube that fit directly into his nostrils. "That better now, Joey?" he asked gently.

Joe and I sat by our son's bed and waited. And, indeed, gradually his groaning grew softer, his heaving chest quieter.

"It doesn't hurt to breathe anymore," he said finally and closed his eyes.

At eleven o'clock that night when three of our church officers stormed the fourth floor determined to be with us in our hour of need, they found Joey and Joe and me all sleeping peacefully.

First Wednesday

Nothing much happened that first Wednesday. Joey had no attacks, and our relief and exhaustion were such that Joe and I just used the time to regroup our forces.

I made myself obnoxious calling friends. "Joey's pain was awful, and it went on and on," I'd say. It seemed the pain had to be shared before it could be forgiven. My description of Joey's pain went on and on, too.

My friends listened like . . . little Christs.

Nor was listening all they did. Some of them had called a special prayer meeting the Monday we brought Joey back to the hospital. And last night some special few had prayed all night long.

Joe ferreted out several Christians, heart Christians, on the hospital staff. How comforting to know they were there, shut right inside those glass and metal enclosures with us. They plied their medical arts to the best of their training and ability, but they put their ultimate trust in something beyond cold x-ray plates and precise laboratory analyses.

"Every day is for the Lord," said the tiniest of the therapists.

And Edie, the social worker, stopped by and touched my shoulder a time or two. "Keep the faith," she said.

I doubt that any of our outside friends or inside friends realized how much they helped us do just that.

First Thursday Morning

My parents have come to stay with Peggie. She adores them both, and what a relief for Joe and me to know Peg is well taken care of. This morning my father drove her over for a visit.

She walked into the room, took one look at Joey, and shot back into the hall sobbing. The head nurse gathered her into her arms. "Oh, Peggie, Peggie," she crooned.

It was a brief storm, however, and when the sun came out it shone more brightly than any sun had shone for many a day.

Peggie was wearing the big blue shoulder bag we'd bought her when she'd gone to Washington with her eighth grade class this past fall, and soon Teddy popped out and she was telling Joey about his latest antics. "Guess what? Teddy has a great-grandfather. I mean, if you're his father, and father is his grandfather, then grandfather must be his great-grandfather, right?"

Joey smiled wanly.

"But you're still his favorite father," she assured him. "He's lonesome without you."

"Who do you think Joey's nurse is today?" I asked.

"Gracie?" Peg squealed. "Oh, you lucky thing, Joey. No bath for you today." Gracie was the one nurse who never got around to giving baths.

"Right," I said. "And if you're very lucky, you may not get your bed changed either."

"Yeah, and if you're very, very, very, very lucky, you may

not have to brush your teeth. Just hope you never get Ann Marie, though. If you get Ann Marie, you end up clean as a cat."

"Meow!" purred Joey. And we all giggled. I couldn't believe Joey and I were sitting there giggling. To what extent had my heaviness been weighing him down, I wondered. I would have to remember what good medicine laughter was, whether Peggie was around or not.

Nancy, another of our favorite nurses, came in then. "Good morning, Peggie. Got a urine specimen for me?"

"I am not a patient," Peg responded indignantly.

"Oh, my mistake," said Nancy. "It's you I'm here for, Mrs. Woodson. Do you have a urine specimen for me?"

Even Joey let out a giant guffaw at that.

First Thursday Noon

I found a place to pray this morning—the university's Newman Club, across the street and down a couple blocks from the hospital. They have mass at 12:15.

What a beautiful service, simple and dignified, Protestant-like in its informality and lay participation. The priest quoted Luther, and I acted Catholic.

It's hard to analyze why it meant so much. Partly, perhaps, because you need a special place to pray when you're living in a hospital. Hospitals are not conducive to privacy; you can only lock yourself in the john for so long.

And partly because I was wearing down, experiencing an inability to concentrate, to close in on God. I needed the discipline and guidance that comes with planned worship.

And I needed to worship with other people, too.

Not that I related personally to anyone at the Newman Club. Most of the students were gone for the summer, and the number at mass was small—everybody but me knowing everybody else and nobody showing any desire to know me. I probably held them off. My emotions billow to the surface when I enter into formal worship. I keep to myself so no one will see if I lose control.

Probably I shouldn't be ashamed of my tears. Probably my tears say more of my love for God and my need of Him than any words could. But I am a reserved person, and when God puts His arms around me, as He does at such times, it's almost more than I can take. If any of His people had put their arms around me, too, I would have been done for.

At any rate, the "Peace be with you" did help. And I did feel at one with the spirit of the group. Christ was with me when I was alone, but something about two or three gathered together intensified His presence. They put it into words in a song they sang:

> Let us break bread together at the altar,
> Break bread together for we are one;
> For when we are together, Christ is with us,
> Break bread together, for we are one.

First Thursday Afternoon

"It's private here in a private room, isn't it, Joey?" I asked this afternoon. Joey had never had a room to himself before.

"Yeah, yeah," he replied. "It's cozy in here."

Dr. Rathburn had meant it when he'd said he was moving Joey to a room of his own so he could get the rest he needed.

Of course, there are times when I feel like a monkey in a cage. Strange how the word spreads when a patient's critically ill. People walking by know they shouldn't look in, but they can't help taking a peek now and then, their vision glazed not so much by pity for us as by a hazy fear that one day they'll be on the inside and somebody else will be out there ogling them.

It's okay, I want to tell them. And I pity them more than they pity me, for there's nothing worse than fears that groan about you unarticulated.

That's one thing I've learned in the last few days—to give form to my fears. Oh, I'm not enamored of them, but every once in a while when pressure builds inside me, I envision what it will be like if Joey dies—when they take his body from the room, the funeral, the house without him, the first day of school in the fall. And I'm finding it's the fears I hide from most frantically that haunt me most efficiently.

I learn from Joey in this. He senses when we've been discussing him. "Hey, tell me how I'm doin'," he demands. "After all, I wanna know, too."

We tell him the truth. Sometimes just part of it, but always the truth. And he always responds in the same way. "Oh," he says simply, satisfied with the simple truth.

Of course, I think it's harder in a way for Joe and me to watch Joey die than it is for Joey to do the dying, but, still, I learn from his total acceptance.

Now Joe rarely asks how Joey's doing. If someone forces him to listen to an almost-sure verdict of death, he hears only the almost. It creates tension between us, for the truth is harder to bear when I have to bear it without Joe.

Yet I must not destroy the solace that is offered with anger for what is not. No one else cares about me or about Joey the way Joe does. I must concentrate more on giving support.

And who am I to feel superior anyway? Probably Joe's right when he says that if I listen to an almost-sure verdict of death, I hear only the sure. Probably I'm not as clear-eyed as I think.

Oh, I look at Joey. I can't take my eyes off Joey, shut up in a cage of his own as he is. Captive to a physical exhaustion that leaves him speechless and emotionless, able to do little but prowl endlessly from one side of the bed to the other.

But what about Dr. Rathburn saying this morning that the longer Joey went without improving the less likely he would ever improve? Have I let myself look at that?

Still, I know I'm on the right track in trying to be half-way honest. Maybe that's why I stopped in the drugstore today on my way back from church and bought this spiral notebook I'm scribbling in now. Admitting to this trauma we're living through on paper will help me admit to it in mind and heart, the past as well as the present and future. I never knew how much you could dread what has already happened, almost more than what is going to happen.

I've finished now recording what I can remember of Friday and Saturday and Sunday—of the happiness of having Joey home and the hell of bringing him back. I've put it to rest. Even the happiness, which is its own specialized kind of damnation now.

I've put it halfway to rest.

First Thursday Night

Nights are awful for me. Bedtimes are disastrous. Today was a good day on the whole, but when darkness fell. . . . Why is it that everything seems black when darkness falls?

Because things are black then? Joey's always worse at night; his symptoms intensify. And I'm worse, too, worn out from the vigil of the day. I know all this, but it's hard to be logical when the time comes. I'm lonely here on this small, white cot. I want my own, normal bed. I want Joe.

Oh, God, will he be here in the morning? Joey, I mean? Will his body still be rising and falling when I peer through the curtains at midnight? At one? At two? Hope eludes me at midnight.

How unreal this thing called night is at the hospital. No one respects strange people who want to sleep. Our linen cabinet is never stocked before nine-thirty. The water is never drained from Joey's nebulizer before ten-thirty. Medications are given at twelve and four. One attendant forgets to close the door when he leaves. The next is careful to shut the door but leaves on the light.

A little aide peered behind my curtain at ten to eleven tonight. "Here's a letter for you, Mrs. Woodson," she called cheerily. Mail delivery at ten to eleven?

"You see, you see," Peggie gloats. "It isn't an easy thing to sleep in a hospital. You think it's my fault when I come home from the hospital tired, but it's not my fault. They keep shining their lights in your face all night long to make sure you haven't gone anyplace."

None of it mattered tonight, because I've been up filling the pages in this notebook. But nighttime still matters.

I remind myself that hospital staff are not the only beings geared to staying up all hours. That the Bible says *He who keeps Israel neither slumbers nor sleeps.*[2]

Will You keep watch while I sleep, Father? Hold Joey tightly through the black hours in Your strong arms? Will You stand by his side, Jesus? Put Your hand on his head and bless him as You blessed the children long ago? Will You, Holy Spirit, breathe into his weak lungs Your love and healing power?

> Now I lay me down to sleep,
> I pray Thee, Lord, my child to keep.

Second Friday Morning

I haven't recorded much that Joey's done the last couple days, but then Joey hasn't done much I can record.

The nurses freshen him up each morning. He eats three meals a day. Four times a day he breathes his aerosol and a therapist drains his lungs. An assortment of hospital staff wander in to draw blood, to collect urine, to do an EKG. Joey is acted upon, but Joey does not act.

"I just wanna rest," he cries in response to every overture. "I just wanna relax." The days run together in the sameness of his fatigue.

It wears me out, the distress I feel at Joey's tiredness. I identify with his weariness to such an extent that my limbs, too, are weighted. But, then, doesn't everything that's ever hurt Joey still hurt me?

I sat beside his bed this morning thinking back to when he'd been in the first grade. He'd gotten to school late one day after the milk money had been collected and taken to the lunchroom. He had to go by himself and order his own milk, a formidable procedure for a six-year-old. Just being late was bad enough.

Joey's own dawdling was responsible; yet I'd grieved over the incident all these years. Joey had been shamed and scared and I had cried. Fortunately for us both, he had known more good times than bad.

Like the St. Patrick's Day in the fourth grade when his teacher had offered a prize for the child wearing the most green items. Joey'd forgotten to mention it till the last minute, but then the whole household had gone wildly Irish. Joey scrambled into dark green pants and bright green shirt. I delved into a box of clothes someone from the church had given us and emerged with two kelly green socks. Peggie pulled the long, white shoelaces from Joe's tennis shoes, magic-markered them forest green, and laced them in Joey's shoes. Joe stuck an olive green pencil behind each of Joey's ears, and off he had trotted, resplendent in his greenness.

He'd strutted into the house that afternoon, shoelaces trailing, the coveted prize held behind his back. It was to be my birthday present, and he had hidden it on top of the refrigerator—a small, green, owl candle. I'd felt golden-green myself that day, Joey's joy of living sprouting from my every pore.

So it came as no surprise now that when Joey groaned in his effort to breathe, my chest hurt. Or that when he lay there immobilized by a languor he could not control, I felt brown, dead with the growing deadness of my beloved son.

Is that one of the things You're trying to tell me, God, when You say You love me as I love Joey? That You identify with me as I identify with him?

I'm scared, Father. It's hard to order your own milk. It's a long walk to the lunchroom. I'm hurting so badly sometimes I think I'll die of hurting before Joey dies of cystic fibrosis.

Are You grieving with me, Father? Is it harder for You to watch me watch Joey die than it is for me to do my watching?

I bowed my head before Him, and it seemed the back of my neck became moist with the flow of His tears. My own tears were quenched by the feel of the hot tears of the Lord on my neck.

Second Friday Noon

The first reading at the Newman Club today was from the prophets. The commentary said that while tradition defines God in terms of masculine power, He is a spirit. He is neither male nor female. And that from time to time in Scripture He compares Himself to a mother: to one who nurtures life, who watches over her children day by day, who mourns over them when they're in trouble, who comforts them with sweet lullabies and gentle kisses.

Well, I was comforted by these thoughts. They gave special worth to my own motherhood, as sorely strained as it was these days.

Patti, a friend of Peggie's from C.F. Camp, is in the hospital. Her mother and I clutch at each other in the hall.

"Is Joey spitting up blood?" she asks.

"A little," I answer, and we join anguishes.

I experience a oneness with mothers of other C.F. children that I experience with no one else. We form a special sorority; no one on the outside understands as well as we initiated ones what another is going through.

Well, almost no one else. The eternal Father-Mother does, of course. Could I think that when He first called down from heaven—"You are my beloved son; with you I am well-pleased"—there was only acknowledgment of His Son in those words? Could I think there was no agony for Himself? I'd been so taken with God's speaking those words to me that I'd forgotten He spoke them first to His only Son.

That He, too, had a Son who was beloved to Him as mine is beloved to me; a Son who pleased Him as my son pleases me; a Son He watched die. He understands what I am going through because He has been through it. I felt newly upheld by my new discernment of what was behind God's empathy.

Then I reversed the process of this morning and I cried for Him. The Lord had always seemed beyond suffering, certainly beyond need of my sympathy. But now I cried for Jesus' Father. I joined anguishes with God.

And then as I thought more about God's saying He loved us not only as a father but as a mother as well, I got thinking, too, about how God also said He loved us as a husband loves a wife. And how Christ said He loved us as a bridegroom loves his bride and as a brother loves a brother and as a friend loves a friend.

Why, there was no relationship of human love the Bible didn't use to give us a tiny intimation of how much God loved us. He said, "You are my beloved son," to me, but to a young husband grieving for a tender, new love He might say, "You are as a beloved bride to me." And to others, "You are my much loved family." Or, "You are my own dear friends."

He's been there weeping, wherever we are in our bereavement, however we've lost a love, for He has lost us all, has He not? All of us whom He has loved so givingly, and not one of us has ever loved Him back in kind.

Second Friday Night

Nancy came in early this morning and talked to me—and I don't mean about urine specimens. We talked about changes in the Catholic church and the role of women in our society, and she didn't feel sorry for me and agree with everything I said.

I cried when Nancy went back to her nursing duties, overcome with the realization of what I've been missing here in solitary confinement, realizing I've been living primarily on feelings for the ten weeks Joey's been sick.

Then I stopped crying and phoned home. "Bring my books when you come today, Joe," I said. "The deep ones. And my writing materials." I gave the poor man an impossible list.

He did a good job with it, though, and so I'm sitting here tonight with one of the toy shelves converted into a book shelf; and with my writing paper and pencils and files of ideas arranged in the window sill; and with the breadboard from the kitchen at home fitting from arm to arm of this easy chair so I can sit next to Joey's bed and write at the same time.

They're not selfish, these promptings toward self-interest. Selfishness, according to my dictionary on the toy shelf, is "having such regard for one's own interests and advantage that the happiness and welfare of others becomes of less concern than is considered right or just."

Well, all the treasures of my life I'd relegate to the junk heap if I could save the treasure buried in that hospital bed.

Joey's condition has moved from critical to guarded. Dr.

Rathburn doesn't think Joey is going to recover, but he does think he may go on as he is for months.

It is for Joey's sake as well as mine that I tend to my own requirements. How much brighter a nurse I am when I satisfy my need to be creative and occasionally treat myself to a luxury or two.

A friend sent a check in a card the other day. "Do with it what you want, Meg," she wrote. "But what I hope you'll do is splurge on yourself." I did. I went out while Joe was here today and had my hair done, and when I went down to the cafeteria tonight I got what I liked best even though it wasn't the cheapest thing on the menu.

When I come in from outdoors, I talk like that's the real world out there. "There's a sun outside," I tell Joey. "It burns through your clothes and the wind blows in your face." Once I brought back a maple leaf and stuck it on his bed.

Yet for me the real world is this room. Strange how time stands still when I leave the hospital. Joey grumbles when I leave. I wish he understood that never, ever do I truly leave him.

Second Saturday Morning

Edie, the social worker, touched my shoulder again when we met in the kitchen yesterday. "Did you know that children who are dying often feel guilty about the trouble they're causing their parents?" she asked.

Now that came as a shock. How could Joey feel bad about my having to take care of him when taking care of him made me so glad?

Well, probably because I had yelled at him so much in years past when he hadn't taken care of himself. "My goodness, Joey, I can't walk into your room at night without taking my life in my hands. Is that some kind of obstacle course you have set up between the door and your bed?"

Yet in taking care of Joey, I had taken care of myself as well. If I hadn't communicated that fact to him before, I would certainly do so now, especially now when doing things for Joey was such an urgent pleasure.

"Isn't this nice?" I asked him last night as I handed him an RC cola, the frantic comings and goings of the day having subsided. "Now there's only me to get things for you."

Then this morning I was helping Nancy give him a manicure, each of us working on one of his hands. "It's important that I sleep at night if I'm going to do things for Joey in the day," I told her. "So last night I asked him to call the nurse when he needed something. Then when I heard the nurse fussing over him, was I ever jealous. How dare she do my job?" Nancy and I laughed together.

Probably Joey didn't have a guilt problem at this point, but if he did, what a simple problem to solve. Would that all his problems could be so simply solved.

I was lost in my books late this morning, so happy to have them again and coming newly alive through them.

"Mama," Joey murmured.

In an instant my breadboard was on the floor and I was bending over him.

"I have a headache, mama."

I ran for a Tylenol, an angelic messenger. Was there any word more beautiful than *mama?*

I wash out Joey's pajamas. I cut up his food. I straighten the room. I weep because there is not more I can do for Joey.

Are you taking a special, urgent pleasure in doing things for me right now, Father?

Is that why You're speaking to me of Your love, because You know that's the best thing You can do for me? That if old love is going to be lost, new love must be available to help fill the emptied spot?

And is that why friends are being so kind to Joey and me here in the hospital and to Joe and Peg at home? And is that why the doctors and nurses are doing a so-much-more-than-is-required-of-them job? Is that the second-best way You have of doing things for us—through other people?

Can I imagine, Father, that Your ear is not always bent to hear me call Your name—Abba? Or that You are not literally moving heaven and earth to answer my call? Is it due to Your effort that I, who always have trouble sleeping under the best of circumstances, have no trouble sleeping now under the worst? My unnatural calm astonishes me. Is it a supernatural calm?

I must not let the one thing You are not doing blind me to the many things You are doing, Father. You may not be giving me my world on a platter, but You have already given me Your world on a cross.[3]

How wonderful to know that You are dedicated to meeting my needs with a deliberation and a discipline and a depth I can only faintly grasp. Thank You, Father, for the high and holy happiness You are experiencing even now in taking care of one of Your children, name of Meg. Thank You for the glad glory that surrounds Your never-ending activity on my behalf.

Second Saturday Night

I sat down tonight in my accustomed spot a yard or so from Joey's bed when he summoned up energy from somewhere and said, "Move the chair over here, mom. I can't see ya so far away. No, closer. Turn it around sideways. Ya know, right up next to me." Then when I had the chair as close to his bed as the law prohibiting two objects from occupying the same space would allow, he patted my arm, "Yeah! Yeah!" he said.

He left his hand hanging through the bedrail, and I folded it close. His fingers intertwined with mine, and he was a puppy dog again, smacking his lips in ultimate contentment.

Now I realize he needs to know I like doing things for him, and that's taken care of. But the best times for both of us are the times I stop doing things for him and am just here touching him in love.

I overslept the other morning. I'd been up late the night before with this diary, and I don't know how long I would have slept if Joey hadn't wakened me with his low rumble: "Hey, when are ya gonna toast my waffles?"

I looked at my watch. Nine o'clock. "Oh, Joey, don't tell me it's that late. How long have you been waiting?"

"Long."

"But why didn't you wake me?"

"I was havin' my aerosol and my therapy. They won't let ya eat before your aerosol and therapy."

"Well, you didn't need me too much then, did you?"

"I wanted ya," he replied.

I felt terrible, not only because I'd let Joey down, but because I had let myself down as well.

I bent and pressed my lips into the hollow of his neck. He was too tired to be handled much, but he lay on his side most of the time, and whenever I pressed my lips into what I had come to think of as our special kissing spot, he hunched his shoulder to cup my face—the best of times.

I sat holding Joey's hand a long time after he went to sleep tonight, holding my son's hand and talking to my Father.

I've always known how I felt about You and me, God, I told Him. I appreciate all the things You do for me. But what I appreciate most are the times You *scoot Your chair* up next to where I am and illuminate my whole being with Your nearness.

And He must appreciate my nearness, too, must He not? Wasn't the enjoyment of another's intimate exchange an integral part of any loving? Was there anything more devastating than love that was not returned? And was any love returned more out of proportion than the love of a child for a father?

Yet I had never let myself think that God and I spending time together meant anything to God.

Even now, when I'm telling myself that God must find the same contentment in *holding my hand* that I find in holding Joey's hand, how I'm underestimating His love.

Is it a blasphemy, Father, for me to compare Your love to mine as I've been doing?

I don't think so, Father. For You are leading me from the known to the unknown, aren't You? And isn't that the only way You can lead me? I wish my mind could stretch far enough to take Your full love in. But this limited mind and heart of mine would burst, would they not, with one split-second recognition of the limitless delight You take in just being close to me?

Second Sunday Morning

God takes into account, I think, not only where a child is spiritually when he dies, but also, given time, what the child would have become. We staked Joey's life on this concept, his eternal life.

Part of us said, push him. Force-feed the Bible into him. Enforce a high code of Christian conduct in response. Make sure he's ready for early death.

We resisted this temptation. We worked hard at Joey's spiritual growth, but we left his total inner response, and much of his outer response, up to him.

We worked particularly hard at our children's attitudes toward death and heaven. "I just can't wait to see Jesus," I'd say enthusiastically. Joey never said much in response. If Joey was anxious to see Jesus, he didn't let on to me. Joey's spiritual growth was slow.

A few weeks before he came down with the measles, we began to work our way through a new book during family discussion, stories of people who testified on their deathbeds to seeing into the next life.

"What do you think about that, kids?" Joe asked one day after a particularly exciting episode.

"I don't think I wanna go to heaven if I have to dance around in an apple orchard all day," said Peg.

"How do ya know they aren't makin' all that stuff up?" asked Joey.

We respected their reactions.

"I mean, people are always talkin' like kids are always runnin' around barefoot in heaven," Peg persisted. "But I don't like to run around barefoot. I don't like to run around in tennis shoes. Have you ever seen one picture of a kid readin' in heaven? If you don't read in heaven, I don't think I wanna go."

"Yeah," Joey echoed. "If ya don't read in heaven, I don't wanna go. And especially I don't wanna go before C.F. Camp."

Yet I think God directed us to use that book through what we didn't know were Joey's last healthy weeks. And I think something of the actuality and allure of heaven seeped in. Else how could he have been unafraid that Tuesday when he expected to die at any moment?

I'm not overestimating him; I don't think he had a burning desire to see God. Yet he had what he needed to have, a conviction deep inside that heaven existed and that it was a kinder place than the troubled bed on which he lay.

One of my primary concerns about Joey has always been his inordinate love of money. Even here, as tired as he is, he insists on doing two things for himself: making out his menu and checking get-well cards for dollars inside. Then I must put the dollars in my wallet, folded in thirds to distinguish them from my money, and when daddy comes I must give them to daddy to put in the skull bank at home.

"Did ya give my dollars to daddy? Did ya, mama?" he perseveres faintly.

"What are you saving all these dollar bills for anyway?" I asked him yesterday.

"A fifty-dollar bill," he replied.

Peggie has always tithed her money conscientiously, more than tithed it really. "I feel cheap givin' God exactly thirty cents out of three dollars," she says. "So usually I give Him another nickel or dime. Sometimes I end up givin' Him a whole dollar."

Joey has never tithed his money conscientiously or any other way. A late bloomer physically, socially, and emotionally, his spiritual immaturity reflects his basic immaturity.

Yet how effortlessly he gave up his dollars when the time came—and to the roof fund.

I went to a Presbyterian church this morning a few blocks away, a magnificent structure shouting eloquently of the mightiness and majesty of God. Just walking inside put things in perspective, the organ thundering the largeness of my Maker clear through me.

And then we rose for the opening hymn:

> Joyful, joyful, we adore Thee,
> God of glory, Lord of love;
> Hearts unfold like flowers before Thee,
> Opening to the sun above.

Relax, my child, God seemed to say. You need not worry about Joey's readiness for heaven. You pointed him to the Sun; you placed him within reach of My rays. And naturally and inevitably he has unfolded to Me.

Second Sunday Night

"I can take anything but the not knowing," I tell Joe repeatedly.

It's true. I am strapped in an emotional roller coaster, rising slowly to heights of insupportable hope, only to drop to despair at sickening speed. The big hills are the worst, but the little ones are bad enough, when they go on and on, when the ride never stops.

On Wednesday morning after last Tuesday—*that Tuesday* —Joey looked at me brightly. "Will you go down to the cafeteria and get me pancakes?" he begged.

I ran. I ran back for a second batch. He wasn't going to die after all. No boy who ate six big pancakes for breakfast could be dying. I listened with wonder as he breathed all day without groaning. Had our giving him to God finally been adequate? Was God now giving him back to us?

"Don't hope too hard," Joe warned. "You know how many times we've seen this happen in the congregation. A family gives up a loved one as dead, and then he rallies. The family mistakes a normal up in the normal up and down course of an illness as an answer to their prayers. Death comes as shock and betrayal." That Tuesday had affected even Joe's eternal optimism.

But I hoped anyway. Joe did, too.

And then the next day those headaches and awful hot spells began. They continue daily. We keep the thermostat so low I sit here huddled in my sweater and trench coat, while Joey lies with his pajama top open refusing even a sheet.

"Turn the heat down some more," he moans. "Tell the nurse to give me something for my headache."

"He doesn't have a fever," Dr. Rathburn says. "Nor are the headaches and hot spells symptomatic of any of his known diseases. Not knowing what causes them, we're at a loss to know what to do about them."

How we dread the onslaught of these mysterious attacks.

And how Joey's increasing fatigue unnerves us. "You can almost see Joey getting more tired day by day," Joe commented to Dr. Rathburn last night. "He used to walk by himself to the bathroom, but now Meg has to hold him up."

"Joey's increasing fatigue is an ominous development," the doctor replied. He had used that word before. Was there any word more ominous than *ominous?*

Doctors, I've discovered, come in all degrees of pessimism and optimism, just like regular people. "His heart doesn't sound too bad," says one. "If we can just get his lungs cleared up now." "I never give up hope . . ." says another, but she leaves the sentence hanging, and the tone in her voice is . . . ominous.

Can't any of you doctors tell me what's going to happen? I accuse them. Are Joey's diseases going to march on their inexorable way or not? Are they going to be arrested by the best medical science can do or not?

The doctors do not know. They cannot predict.

But I have to know—now.

Just a couple hours ago Joey had another spell when he couldn't breathe. "Air! Air!" he gasped.

Fear, I've decided, is the most primitive of human emotions.

Can't You tell me what's going to happen, God? I accuse Him. Are Joey's diseases going to be arrested by the best Your love and power can do or not? Don't You know either? Can't You predict?

Forgive me, Lord. I know You know all things. But we can't

predict Your ways, can we? It's one of our biggest faults, trying to psych out Your Godness. We take all we know about Your characteristics, about the way You have dealt with Your people through history, about Your promises, about our need. We feed it all into our finite minds and compute Your one, inevitable response.

But You are infinite. And He is a tiger, that Christ of Yours. He stalks unpatterned jungles, while we insist on strolling safe, well-trodden paths. No wonder we scaredy-cats have trouble walking with Him.

Is that what You want of me right now—to charge this alien darkness? Is it a higher kind of surrender, higher even than surrendering to certain death—surrendering to uncertainty? Is it a higher kind of trust, higher even than trusting You for life—just trusting You?

Second Monday Morning

Things quiet down in the hospital on weekends. Beds empty out. Labs close. I had time to look at myself the last couple days, and I didn't like what I saw.

I woke up this morning deeply distressed. And not over Joey. No, the awfulest sight I've seen since Joey's been in the hospital is not the sight of his wasted body but of my wanton spirit. All that happens to Joey I view primarily from the perspective of my need.

I've been painting myself in this diary like some kind of perfect mother, and it's true that a part of me weeps because there is not more I can do for Joey. It's true that a part of me longs to hear him call my name, night and day. But when he does, it's also true that a part of me snaps, Oh, no, not again, Joey. Can't you see I'm writing? For goodness sakes, what now, Joey?

And on occasion I actually catch myself thinking. . . . No, I cannot put on paper the thoughts I occasionally catch myself thinking.

Forgive me, Joey.

And, then, right in the middle of my depression I remembered a report on India Joey'd had to write in the fifth grade, particularly one question he'd had to answer: "If you were traveling to Calcutta, what means of transportation would you use, and what would you see along the way?"

Joey'd had no trouble with that one. "If I was traveling to

Calcutta," he scrawled, "I would travel in a air-conditioned plane. I would mostly see clouds."

"The teacher can't mark him wrong for that," Peg conceded. "He gave her exactly what she asked for."

Well, I marked him wrong in no uncertain terms. Joey was far too adept at evasion maneuvers, and delaying tactics, and in generally getting his own lazy way. Still, when I'd been by myself, I'd had to chuckle.

Once he had shut a friend up in our basement. The boy had screamed, first in anger and then in fright, but the louder he screamed, the harder Joey threw his weight against the basement door.

"Whatever made you do a thing like that?" I asked him later.

He said he didn't know. Do any of us know why we try with all our might to hurt those we love? I didn't laugh at the basement incident.

The point was, though, that even as I was scolding Joey I was loving him. I so urgently wanted him to do right: the aching love I felt for him when he did wrong was the strongest love of all.

Is that the way You as a Parent feel toward me when I sin, Father? I asked.

But no easy answer came. For the church of Christ had worked hard through the years at making me good by shouting at me how bad I was. It had not worked.

God loves you, sinner, they said, but. . . . They always followed the words with a but, and they emphasized the sinner. You can see nothing but evil, they said. Hear nothing but evil. Speak nothing but evil. God loved me—but never because of anything I was, only in spite of everything I was. God's love became a monkey on my back.

Yes, a frightful me-firstness shadowed Joey's mind, his heart, his will. My flesh, my spirit. Yes, there was something awful about mankind that forced God to give His Son to save it.

But by the same token there had to be something awfully worth saving. Some beauty, darkened by ugliness, but beauty nonetheless. Some conscience in the midst of all the callousness. Some goodness.

Do You notice when I sin humorously, Father? Or cleverly? Or sensitively? Not that You ever find my self-worship cute, but do You at times admire the remnant of Your image left in me even when I'm using it to avoid responsibility?

Is it when I sin the worst that You love me the most? When I lock my brother in the basement? When I lock my dying son out of my heart? Is that when You yearn over me most earnestly, as You yearned over the prodigal son, the son who ran away? In a air-conditioned plane? To the dark hole of Calcutta?

Thank You, Father, for not requiring me to be a saint to be the recipient of Your love. I don't need to hide any part of me from Your awareness. I never realized how much I needed someone to know me altogether. To know me and not turn away.

If You, my Father, find me lovable, then I must be lovable. Then I will become lovable. Even me, Your dear, deadly sinner, Meg.

Second Tuesday Morning

First thing this morning I sang out to Joey the news Dr. Rathburn had just given me. "Your heart is back to normal size, Joey."

"Oh," said Joey.

I didn't tell him his liver was back to normal, never having told him it was enlarged. But it was. His heart and his liver were both back to normal size.

"And your kidneys are doing great, too, Joey."

He seemed as tired as he had right along, wanting nothing but to lie there and roll from side to side undisturbed. But I could not help myself; I dared to think Joey might get well.

I arranged myself next to his bed with my books and note pad as usual. It wasn't easy for me to concentrate on anything but Joey this morning, my son who might not die. But I made a stab at it, looking up the "beloved son" verse in all the translations of the Bible Joe had brought me, and writing my own composite translation: "You are my own dear, much-loved Son—my beloved Son. Yes, you are my delight. I take much pleasure in you."

I could not leave out any endearment. I spoke every endearment to Joey, and the Lord spoke every endearment to me.

Next I looked up all the other verses on God's love I could find. The thing that struck me, naturally enough, was the permanency of God's love. God's love for me went on and on—endlessly—both ways.

It seemed incredible that God always had loved me. Yet the Bible said that God had purposed that I would be His son— because of His love—before the world was made.[4]

And the Bible also said that God always would love me, that nothing could ever separate me from God's love—neither death nor life; neither the present nor the future; not anything in all creation.[5]

My love for Joey had had a beginning—the moment the doctor had said, "You have a fine boy, Mrs. Woodson," and held Joey's scrawny body high. And though now I liked to think that if Joey died I would love him as fervently fifty years from now as I loved him at this moment, I knew that memories would dim in time.

This morning, however, I did not believe Joey was going to die, not soon. But even this morning I knew that human love came with impermanence built in, subject to termination by gradual indifference or sudden betrayal. Or, if by nothing else, soon or late, by the ultimate certainty of life, death.

Yet how we humans long for someone whose love is forever, never tiring of us, always present for us. Well, there has never been a moment in time past when I have not existed in the heart of God. Nor will there be such a moment time without end. Amen.

Second Tuesday Afternoon

I stayed settled down beside Joey this afternoon. I could not leave him, my son who might yet grow into a man. Nor could I leave my books, for this afternoon I discovered that God's love not only moved Him to do things for me, but compelled Him to do basic, beautiful things through me. God's love was committed to all I might become.

One of our favorite family pastimes before Joey got sick was playing four-handed solitaire. The only thing that blighted the wild fun of these games, for three of us, was that Joey could keep every card on the table in his mind at once and move his own cards so quickly that the rest of us didn't have a chance. Joey won so often and gloated so loudly that Joe began putting an ice cube down his back after every game—to teach him humility.

Not that we really wanted to inhibit him. How we longed to see him grow, to develop in whatever field he chose to make his contribution, to be able to see things whole and make the correct moves, not for boasting but for serving.

What patience Joey had, and what fine precision of mind and hand. He could take anything apart; he designed and put together the most intricate contraptions. We praised his talents to the skies. We provided opportunities for him to develop every skill he possessed.

A couple summers ago he had attended a YMCA day camp—ended up Honor Camper, as a matter of fact. One thing he did was not honorable, though—gobbling up a whole bag of potato chips, a coveted prize of some sort.

He wasn't supposed to eat greasy foods, and that night he had a rectal prolapse, a painful happening where the rectum turns inside out and hangs on the outside. Joe took him to the emergency room of the nearest hospital. Three doctors came and went before one came who knew how to put Joey's rectum back in.

Then this past year he had bounded into the house one afternoon after school, dumped down his books, and started out to play. But then he had run back in. "Oh, yeah, mom," he said. "When I was in the bathroom in school today, that thing came on the outside again."

"My goodness, Joey, what did you do?"

"Well, it took twenty minutes, but I squeezed and squeezed and I finally got it back in."

He was out the door again, but then back in once more, shaking his finger teacher-like in my face. "With God's help!" he added solemnly.

I had cried to think of him in the bathroom so long by himself, hurting and squeezing and praying, but the tears had been partly tears of pride and hope. Fond hope that one day he would be a fine grown man, in control, able to endure whatever pain might come his way—with God's help!

How I wanted to keep on pouring myself into the Honor Person to come and watching him become it. It was such a basic part of loving him.

And it was a basic part of God's loving me, too. How much it meant to realize this, for how poignantly the desire to amount to something drum-rolls within the human breast. To be good and to be good for something, what more do we want from life?

That we be pure and that we be productive, what more does God want for us? That's what the whole Bible is, the story of God's providing for our salvation.

Most times in the past when I'd asked Joey what he wanted

to be when he grew up, he had shrugged. But once he surprised me by saying, "Maybe a minister like my father."

Peg had shrieked with laughter. "Him a minister?" Peg had doubled over laughing. But I had not laughed.

Maybe you'll be a minister yet, I told Joey silently this afternoon.

How strangely he breathed these days. His chest remained flat, almost unmoving, but how deeply his stomach pumped. "It's good he's working so hard," Dr. Rathburn tells me. And this afternoon even the eerie way he breathed seemed good.

God did not give His Son for me so He could own me, mechanize me.[6] God gave His Son for me that I might become like His Son,[7] the Son through whom He made the world[8]—powerfully and creatively alive.[9]

It was no weak sentiment, God's love for me. Nor did it lead to weakness in me. All that God was, for as long as God was, God was for the making of me.

Second Wednesday Afternoon

"I can't walk to the bathroom, mom," Joey said this afternoon. "I'm just too tired."

Dot was in the room at the time. "Of course you can, Joey," she retorted. "You never will get well if you lie there in that bed all the time."

But when Dot left, Joey was adamant. "Carry me, mama. Please carry me."

Carefully I moved everything between his bed and the bathroom on which his oxygen cord might catch, and I lifted him in my arms. How long it had been since I held him. I bound him to me.

Then when I'd gotten him back to bed I tracked down Dr. Rathburn.

"Joey's increasing fatigue fits," Dr. Rathburn said, his eyes avoiding mine for the first time. "Joey's carbon dioxide was up last night."

Some inborn alarm system, ancient as motherhood, sickened my stomach. "What do you mean his carbon dioxide was up?"

When finally I returned to the room, I walked past Joey's bed and stood staring out the window. The moisture on my cheeks seemed a mixture of the drizzle and smog below. What it meant was that my hopes of yesterday had been illusions. Dr. Rathburn was more willing to predict now, to predict no turning back.

What it meant was that while Joey might not be on his way to dying of heart failure, he was on his way to dying of respiratory failure.

I looked away from the parking lot and up to bleak skies above. I tried to ask the Lord how He could do this to me if He loved me. I tried to rail against Him—don't You care? But I could not, for the knowledge most basic to my being was that He did care. He had fixed it so that I could not cut myself off from His strength had I wanted to.

Daily trips to the hospital were wearing Joe out, and this afternoon my father drove him over and sat with Joey while Joe and I went down to the cafeteria for supper.

"Joey's carbon dioxide is up because his lungs can't handle the amount of oxygen he's getting," I explained.

"Why don't they lower the oxygen?"

"He'd have those spells when he can't get enough air again, and eventually . . . he'd die of too little oxygen. It's better . . . he die of too much carbon dioxide because it will be less painful. He'll grow more and more . . . groggy . . . till finally he'll be unconscious. He'll be unconscious . . . when he dies." I was trying to be brave, but my voice would not cooperate.

"But Joey's lungs were never that bad, Meg."

"I know. I know. But the heart and lungs are interrelated. Joey's lungs deteriorated a lot while his heart wasn't functioning normally."

"How long does he have?" For Joe, Joe was asking a lot of questions, and his voice was cracking, too.

"Maybe weeks. Maybe not."

I told Joe what I'd been learning about the beloved son business then. I tried to comfort him with my comfort, but I could tell it didn't mean to him what it meant to me.

He said nothing in response, but he held my eyes ever so gently across the table and placed his hand over mine where it lay between our coffee cups. "I sure am glad I'm married to you, Meg," he said. "You sure do mean a lot to me."

I could say nothing back.

One of the interesting facts I uncovered yesterday was that

God said "You are my beloved Son" to Jesus on two separate occasions—before the long, extensive trial of His ministry and before the brief, intensive trial of His crucifixion.

I found myself asking if God was lacking in originality. Could He think of nothing better to say? And I found myself answering, No, He could think of nothing better to say.

When Joe spoke to me this afternoon in that plain, honest way of his, "I sure am glad I'm married to you," I thought, What if he doesn't understand what I understand or vice versa? He loves me. What do I need to understand more than that?

So when I hear God say, "I sure am glad you're My daughter, Meg. I sure do love you," I think, God is giving me the best He can give me. God is giving me Himself.

I still don't know the answers to the whys I asked that first Monday night in the cafeteria; I would still like to know. But I do not have to know. As long as I know that the things that are happening are not happening because God does not love us, I do not have to know.

We have not depended on made-up legends [said the apostle Peter] in making known to you the mighty coming of our Lord Jesus Christ. With our own eyes we saw his greatness. We were there when the voice came to him from the Supreme Glory, saying, "This is my own dear Son, with whom I am well-pleased!" . . . You will do well to pay attention to it like a lamp shining in a dark place. . . .[10]

Second Thursday Morning

Joey seemed especially tired this morning, especially *groggy*. That word unglues me, that word Dr. Rathburn used to describe worst coming to worst.

I was all too aware this morning that surrender is not a once-in-a-lifetime thing. I could not give myself one shot, offer one prayer of commitment of all that was dear to me to the will of God, and achieve permanent immunity to wanting my own way.

The nurses came in this morning to say "Hi" the way they do every morning when the shifts change. "How are you doing today, Joey?" they asked.

"Oh, pretty good," Joey replied, the way he has all along when anybody's asked him how he was doing. He didn't seem to think he felt any different. "Who's my nurse today?"

A little later one of the therapists asked me how I was getting along.

"Oh, pretty good," I found myself responding with exactly the inflection Joey had used. Now which of us had picked that up from the other? Not only did Joey have my eyes and my hair, but my spirit as well.

Is that part of what man's being made in Your image means, Father? That as earthly parents cherish the reflection they see of themselves in their children, You cherish the likeness to Yourself You see in us?

Joey will take a good bit of me with him if he dies, Father.

Please don't let anything separate us. But mostly, Father, please don't let anything separate Joey from Your best plan for him—not all the demons of hell, nor all the prayers of all the saints, nor routine hospital carelessness, nor medical expertise, nor my own relentless delight in the form and feel of him. Let me never give up giving him up to You.

I've been thinking too much about Your love for me. *I* love *You,* Father. Please, Father, all that I am for as long as I am, let me be in obedience to You.

Second Thursday Afternoon

I have taken to walking tall these days, head high, shoulders back. It makes walking down the hall an exercise of soul as well as body. How easy it is to slouch; yet it's easy to walk upright, too.

They took Joey down to x-ray this afternoon, in a wheelchair with an oxygen tank on the back. They put a pillow in the chair, and he collapsed against it in a heap. They will not let me take him by myself. He has to go with an attendant, who has to round up five or six other children on the way, so it's in and out of elevators and locating each child and waiting for each child and then waiting for Joey's turn when we get there.

The ordeal wears him out to such an extent that I rage at whoever it is in this place of endless routines who imposes this senseless routine on him.

Today, though, it was easy to walk tall even going to x-ray, for Bob, the six-footer in the room next to ours, was walking with us. Nobody knows much about cystic fibrosis but pediatricians, and the pediatricians here are not about to throw their patients out when they outgrow childhood, so C.F.ers even in their twenties and thirties are admitted to Babies and Childrens Hospital.

"Know where I can find a nurse when I can't find one anyplace else?" I whispered to Joey. "In Bob's room giving Bob back rubs. That Bob has got to have the best-rubbed back on the whole fourth floor."

Joey nodded knowingly.

"Bob doesn't get all the special attention, though. Know how you write 'steak-rare' on your menu every night? Well, Bob writes steak in on his menu every night, but he never gets it. The nurses say when he sees it on your tray he turns green with envy."

I started to complain to Joe later in the day about Joey's hard time going to x-ray, but before long Joe had us all sitting around listing things we were grateful for instead. Something to do with a verse in the Bible about giving thanks at all times, in all circumstances.

"I thank God for the dietician," said Joey, as well he might.

"I thank God for all hospital personnel who think of people first and rules second," I said.

"I thank God for such a good hospital for Joey to be in, and that I'm able to be here today with him and mama," Joe said.

How this most positive of all thinking strengthened my physical being.

"I thank God for being able to thank God," I said. For being able to walk tall inside and out, I added to myself. For matter over mind, and for mind over matter.

Second Thursday Night

Dr. Rathburn said Joey's carbon dioxide went up another couple points tonight. It seems this thing often develops a rhythm, every couple days another couple points.

I picked up a devotional book when the doctor left. "Worry is a sin," said the devotional book in an unqualified statement of fact. I felt the chief of sinners.

Yet I know a peace exists alongside my anxiety. Certainties nestle down inside me beyond the reach of any disquietude.

I will have more than my own strength to face whatever happens. A tranquillity lies inherent in the knowledge that Christ will be with me whatever happens. And I know where Joey is going if the worst happens. And that's serenity—knowing where Joey's going.

And I know where I'm going, too. Part of me will die with my child. I'll not fight that. But resurrected life will follow.

I could pretend that I know nothing but peace. But straining and acting like nothing is bothering me when my insides are churning, would that be peace or hypocrisy?

I love God. All my other desires are integrated into that love. The core of me is impregnable because of that love. An inner harmony sings with that love.

But I do worry. And anyone who tells me it's a sin has never stood where I stand, looking down at my beloved son with that awful pumping in his middle and the gray of the corpse on his face.

Third Friday Noon

I had an awesome time at church today, dedicating the whole service to a celebration of God.

I gave God acclaim for all He was as I had come to know Him, for His love and power and goodness and mercy and truth and on and on. I applauded Him for every way I could remember in which His love and power had been operative in my behalf. I adored Him for all He was that I did not or could not grasp and for all the ways He worked on my behalf of which I had no knowledge.

I was beside myself over Joey, but I did not on this occasion say, "Heal my child." I did not even say, "Your will be done in my child." Or, "Give me strength for whatever happens to my child." And yet, when I rose from praise, my universe was right side up.

Now I do not extol God for the good that accrues to me. I extol Him because it is in accord with the purpose of my being to extol Him. Yet God does dwell in the praises of His people. And I found today, as so many before me have found, that our most need-meeting prayers are not those in which we concentrate on getting something from God but those in which we concentrate on giving something to Him.

I confess I did make one petition. It was in accord with the spirit of praise, however, and it is inside me all the time whether or not it comes out in spoken words. The petition was that Joey, too, would praise the Lord. That above all else Joey would, in life or death, glorify the Lord.

And when I prayed that . . . Ah, the whole process of man's giving glory to God reversed itself, and God turned and let His glory shine on me.

Third Saturday Morning

I woke this morning to the ringing of the phone. "I just wanna know one thing, mother," Peggie's voice rasped. "Am I gonna get a bike or am I not gonna get a bike?"

"What brought this on, Peg?" I asked drowsily.

"Well, I been thinkin'. How long has it been since you told me I could have a new bike? I mean, I bet you don't even remember how long it's been so long." And then before I could reply, she slammed the receiver in my ear.

I slumped back on my pillow. If there was one thing I didn't need today, it was an adolescent. Yet I knew what I was hearing was more than the normal fluttering of a young girl trying her woman's wings, for Peggie's only brother lay dying—and of the same disease Peggie had.

"Daddy keeps snapping at me," she complained one day.

"Well, you have to understand how worried daddy is, Peggie. He's bound to be a little on edge."

"But what about me?" she exploded. "Doesn't anybody think I worry? You talk to me with your voice all bright and cheery, but I know what you're doin'. Don't you think I know what's goin' on?"

If I didn't tell Peggie about Joey's condition, she upbraided me for that. But if I tried to tell her, she hung up the phone. Never had she acted like that.

It wasn't that Peggie didn't try to be thoughtful. One day I gave her a long list of things to pack for me. She found every one and tucked in a few extras besides, like her camp soap dish with a bar of the scented soap she had given me for my birthday inside.

Another time she sent a cheer-up note.

Hello Mama,

How are you doing? I'm glad you're sleeping good! I sure do miss you! Maybe if I can get rid of my cold sometime soon, then I can come see you. Do you need any reading material? I got a book called *Maria* about Maria Von Trapp from *The Sound of Music*. It's very interesting. Well, I have to go. We're going out to eat for Sunday dinner.

See ya.

I love you.

> Love,
> Peggie ☺

I don't know what I would do without Peggie's sunny visits. Even her girlish confidences, distracting me as they do, comfort me as nothing else—save the feel of her skinny arms around my waist.

It's not that Peggie doesn't try hard. And it's not that I don't try hard either.

Joey has been receiving get-well cards by the fistful, so I went down to the Hospitality Shop last week and bought Peggie a card with a big smiley-face heart on the front and a verse that said my heart was smiling because she lived inside.

When she comes to the hospital, I make a point of going down to the cafeteria with her, just the two of us, or we sit together on my cot behind the curtain. I call her frequently on the phone. Yet things like this bike bit come up persistently.

I keep thinking of a television show I saw some time ago. A pioneer mother was confined to a log cabin with three small, sick children. The father had been ambushed by Indians. A possum stole the last scrap of food in the house. In desperation the mother sent an older child fishing. Hours later the child returned, empty-handed, except for a collection of colored stones. She had forgotten to fish.

Well, young people are like that. Inherently carefree, it's hard for them to maintain a sensitivity to the tension around them for any period of time.

Peggie called early in the morning yesterday, too. "What should I wear today, mother?" she clamored. Now it's summertime, and it doesn't matter what she wears. She stopped insisting I make these decisions for her a couple years ago. But on and on she went, whining, fault-finding.

Well, young people are like that, too. It's hard for them to react to the tension around them from any but a selfish, demanding perspective.

Not that we older folks are any better. Oh, I made concessions with Peggie on the phone yesterday. "How about your bib shorts and green shirt?" I asked.

"Oh, mother, those old things?"

I kept trying, but even I could hear the edge in my voice. How can you do this to me, Peg? it was screaming. Don't put this burden on me right now.

It is hard for older folks to react to the tension around them from any but a selfish, long-suffering perspective.

I try to give Peggie all my attention when we go down to the cafeteria, but she keeps waving her hand in front of my eyes. "Just testing, mother," she says.

It is hard for older folks to react to anything but the tension around them.

The phone rang again just now, but this time Peg's voice was ecstatic. "I got it! I got a bike. It's pale blue and three speeds. Daddy was gettin' ready to go to the hospital, but all at once he changed his mind. I mean, I didn't ask him to or anything, and he was already in the car, but all at once he changed his mind and took me to the bike store instead, and I got it. I got a bike! Put the phone up next to Joey's ear, will you, mother?"

"I explained they had a boy's bike to match mine," she told me soberly when I took the phone back. "And I asked him did he want to get it when he came home, and I know he liked the idea 'cause he said 'Yeah, yeah' that way he does.'' Her voice broke then.

"The only thing is . . .'' she went on shakily, "I'm not so sure pale blue . . . is such a good color for a . . . oh, mama. Mama.''

Third Saturday Night

"Joey insisted his oxygen wasn't coming through, and everybody else insisted it was," I told Dr. Rathburn yesterday. "Then when Joey had gotten hysterical and everybody else had given up, I found that his oxygen cord had come apart under the bed. All the oxygen was pouring out on the floor."

Dr. Rathburn shook his head. "Hospitals are awful places," he said.

He's said that all through the years whenever I've complained about anything. "The best thing you can do is get out of here as soon as possible. Hospitals are awful places."

Now I have been in other hospitals. I am convinced that no other hospital is as fine as this hospital. Yet a certain dreadfulness went up along with the brick and steel of even this structure. It is built into what any hospital is here for and what it can and cannot do.

All kinds of people who would have nothing to do with each other in the outside world are thrown into constant contact here. Three or four rushed nurses can only give twenty-five children so much love. A fallible staff functions in situations demanding infallible behavior.

Children holler in pain in hospitals.

Children with bodies shrunken by disease; bodies broken by parents; mutilated by technology; burned. The burns are so bad.

"Everybody out of the hall," barks Dot. "Come on, you guys.

I said everybody back to their rooms."

"What's the matter with her?" a boy across the hall asks his friend. "We wasn't doin' nothin'."

Soon a stretcher carrying its sheet-shrouded load is wheeled quickly down the hall.

Children die in hospitals.

Even as I am writing this, Large Larry is at it again. If there were not a wall between this room and the ward next door, Large Larry's bed and my cot would meet head to head. Now Large Larry roars. He isn't in pain, but his roaring has such an anguished, rhythmic quality, you would swear the Gestapo was working him over.

Sometimes when I'm lying in bed like this at night and Large Larry is in good form it seems like all the pain that has tortured human beings throughout all history is roaring through my head.

The babies in the maternity hospital down the street are a different story, Lord, soft and sweet, reflecting in their innocent newness something of what life must have been like as You originally made it. Forgive us for spoiling things rotten, Lord. Forgive our original sin. And forgive our persistent uncaringness, our careless efforts at restoration.

> Lord, have mercy on our souls.
> Christ, have mercy on our bodies.
> Lord, have special mercy on our children's bodies.

Third Sunday

It is not easy losing a child, regardless of the state of surrender you are in, or how tall you walk, or what truth the Lord has given you to see you through.

And Sundays are as bad as nights.

I went out to church this morning. That got me started crying, and I have not been able to stop since. And I thought I was doing so well. Everybody comments on how well I'm doing. But here I am crouched behind my curtain at midnight still crying and aching all over. It is so cold in this room. I cannot stop shaking tonight.

Friends stopped in after church. They brought their sons along—the younger one, Gary, a friend of Joey's from school as well as Sunday school. His father pushed him forward, and he walked up to the still, oxygen-masked form on the bed as though he were approaching death itself. Which he was.

"Hi, Joey," he said, and tears rushed to my eyes at the fear in his voice. Joey on occasion may have been afraid of Gary, but never had Gary been afraid of Joey.

I got him talking about his baseball team, and his big brother explained procedures for the first day at junior high. Gary had run in and out of our house for years, but how uncomfortable he was with us now, even in his tennis shoes and with his hair going every which way. He's sprouting up, his mother says.

Tomorrow will be the first of July. Boys ought never to die in July. July is when boys pack provisions in old school lunch boxes and scramble down to the creek on African safaris. And mothers worry about snakes. And boys come back scratching all over and smelling like it's time they used a deodorant.

July is when boys take off shirts and shoes and run through the grass on tender feet with the wind smacking their chests and the sun broiling their backs. July is the month for body life.

July is the month for family life. I have already told Joe there is one place I cannot go this summer, if we go anyplace, and that is back to Fire Island. Too many ghosts would be building sand castles on Fire Island; too many shadows in yellow trunks would be streaking through the waves.

How could we go anyplace as a family this summer without Joey? Without Joey we would not be a family.

All through the years, no matter how busy I've been the rest of the week, late Sunday afternoons have belonged to the children.

Well, I got Joey to watch Walt Disney with me this afternoon. I bribed him with Cracker Jacks, even though I didn't know how high they were in sodium. I always fixed special treats at home when we watched television on Sundays, and this afternoon I put a few Cracker Jacks on a plate for Joey and a few on a plate for me and pulled my chair up close to him all snuglike.

He lasted through five minutes of "The Wild Mustang" before he rolled over whimpering with fatigue. "All I wanna do is relax," he cried.

Oh, God, I tempted him with forbidden fruit—and to his detriment.

A small boy with brown hair and glasses keeps trotting down the hall. Every time I see him it gives me a jolt. Just for a minute I think it's Joey the way he was in previous hospitalizations, tearing from the playroom to the poolroom, to the cafeteria, to the Hospitality Shop. Sometimes we went exploring in the underground tunnels and made believe we were lost. Sometimes we were lost.

I read a book once by a father whose teen-age son died. He

said that for months afterward every time he saw a teen-ager driving a car, elbow resting on the sill, his eyes misted and he had to pull off the road.

Well, I know what will do it for me. Small, brown-haired boys frisking about in shorts—especially on Sundays—in July.

Third Monday Morning

When I came back from the Parents' Lounge this morning and saw Joey lying so still, just for a moment I thought he was up to one of his old tricks.

Whenever I had come to see him during his last hospitalization, he had laid that way, making believe he was asleep.

"Hi, Joey," I'd say, rattling my shopping bag enticingly. "I have some surprises here for you, but if you're asleep maybe I should give them to your roommate."

No response.

"Yummy. These blueberry muffins I made you taste pretty good. Think I'll have another."

Not a quiver.

"Well, guess I may as well be going," I'd say finally, heading for the door.

"Oh, hi, mom," Joey would cry, suddenly *waking*. "I didn't know you were here." He had never tired of playing this game.

I should have known better this morning, known he was too tired to play any game. The tiny incident knocked the wind out of me, and I sat down beside Joey and got to reminiscing about his fondness for corny jokes, as Peggie calls them.

The sixth grade boys had learned to knit this year, and on April Fool's Day Joey had taken his plastic snake and hidden it in his knitting bag. Then he'd asked his regular teacher to look at the rug he was making, and obligingly she had put her hand in the bag.

"What did Miss Murdock say, Joey?" we asked.

"She said for me to go do it to the knitting teacher."

"Well, what did the knitting teacher say?" We always had to pull every bit of information out of him.

"She said, 'Joey, you're rotten clear through.'"

I had been inclined to agree with the knitting teacher that day. Every time I shut one kitchen drawer, the drawer next to it popped open. Cabinet doors were fastened shut. Chair legs were tied together. Had all that happened just three months ago today?

I don't suppose we could have Joey back like his old self for just another year, could we, Father? Or even six months? A week perhaps? I knew I was tormenting myself unnecessarily, but all through the early morning I sat beside Joey's bed wrapped in my trench coat and in my memories of how things used to be—and in my longing for them to be that way again. I made myself sick with longing.

And then mid-morning I read through some piled-up mail, one of the letters a response to an article I had written months before on how I had learned to live with cystic fibrosis. "Don't you know, Mrs. Woodson?" the writer asked. "Haven't you heard that God is healing today? You don't have to live with cystic fibrosis. Have faith. Your children don't have to be sick."

Don't you know what you are doing to me? I wailed in response. Haven't you heard that the one thing parents of a critically ill child cannot bear, even on a physical level, is to know that everything that can be done for their child is not being done? If Joey doesn't have to be dying, and yet he is, what kind of killer does that make me?

The letter reminded me of an acquaintance who had come to visit a couple days before. "The Lord told me to come to see you," she said, and proceeded to tell me about a speaker she had heard the previous night. It seems his wife had been in an accident and the doctors had given up on her, said if she lived she would be a vegetable. But the speaker had prayed for her, and she had opened her eyes and talked to him *just like her old self.*

It was hard for me to believe the Lord had sent this woman. If the Lord had sent her, she would have stopped talking and let me share some of the things He had been teaching me. It would have helped if she would just have let me share my tears.

"It's like I'm a starving man," I cried to Joe later in the morning, "and they tell me bread is just around the corner. But when I race around the corner, there is no bread there. They have no right to invade my private, desperate longings and work such desolation there. We believe in healing, Joe. No one's prayed for healing more than we."

"But if it's as automatic as they make it, why don't they pray Joey well? And if they can't, why don't they get off my conscience?"

Joe led me down to the Parents' Lounge. "Remember the things we've learned, Meg, about even faith being a gift of God? These people have hold of a part of a truth, but only a part. Yes, faith can move mountains, but only when God wants the mountain moved and gives the faith for that purpose."

Joe put his arm around me, and I leaned up against him and wept. We sat that way for quite a while, neither of us saying anything. Strange how much the solid touch of him helped.

"They talk with such an infallible air, Joe," I said at length. "They equate their own voices with the voice of God."

"You can't rely on what anybody else thinks God is saying to you, Meg," Joe replied. "Trust your own judgment. Rely on what you feel God has taught you."

Joe left to get back to Joey then, but I stayed behind remembering some of the things I felt God had taught me in the past few days about my being His much-loved child.

One of the commentaries I'd read said that while the entire sentence "You are my beloved Son with whom I am well-pleased" was a quotation from the Old Testament, the first half, "You are my beloved Son," came from a part of the Old

Testament that referred to the messianic King. And the second half, "In you I am well-pleased," came from a part describing the suffering Savior.

So even as God spoke of His love for His Son in these words, He was assuring Him of horrors as well as honors to come.

Why should I expect my sonship to guarantee me only happy events? It was the heresy of the present-day church—the defining of sonship as protection from every pain and provision of every pleasure.

"My Father, if it is possible, take this cup away from me! But not what I want, but what You want," I prayed as God's Son had prayed before me on His way to His cross. And the peace of God came pouring in with that praying.

But how quickly I forgot. For the Gospel reading at mass this noon told the story of the raising of Jairus's daughter from the dead. "She isn't dead," Christ said. "She's sleeping."

"Well, that is all fine and good," I said. "But Joey isn't sleeping; Joey isn't even playing that he's sleeping; Joey's dying. Why don't You do what You said You would do?" I demanded of the Lord. For a minute I believed the voices of men when they said because God was my Father I could have anything I wanted for the asking.

Forgive me, Father. And help me forgive those of Your children who add to my ordeal. They mean well, and they are Your children, many of them closer to You than I. It's just that I could not breathe in the universe of a God who did not keep His promises.

Third Monday Afternoon

We talked to the doctor again this afternoon. We didn't ask any questions we had not already asked. "Does Joey have any chance at all? How long does he have?"

Nor did we get any answers we had not already gotten. "I don't think so. Maybe a week or two. Maybe a few months."

Only this time we heard the answers. At least I did. For the first time I saw it beginning to end, this drama in which Joe and Peggie and I play prominent roles, in which Joey plays the leading role. And it was no playacting any of us were doing. We were starring in a real-life production—and a tragedy at that.

I realize I have talked right along like I believed Joey was going to die. But I have never fully believed it, except perhaps for a few hours on that first Tuesday. It was my way of preparing for the worst that might happen. And I am not saying even now I fully believe it. Part of me still hopes for a surprise ending, will hope every suspenseful moment till the curtain falls.

But basically I have moved from surrender of whatever God's will might be for Joey to a considered acceptance of death as His will—the most tortured step I have ever taken. Yet I feel untortured for having taken it.

Refusal to say the lines the Author has written for you is not faith; it is violation of contract.

It's hard to pinpoint what convinced me that death was in God's script for Joey. Partly, I'm sure, the thoughts I've had about the validity of suffering in the life of the Christian.

I wish I could say I asked the Author-Director-Producer to reveal His plot and that He previewed for me everything to come. I can say I asked Him, but I cannot say I got an answer.

All I can say is that I had to take this step. Surrendering to obscurity is a high form of surrender—for a while. But the human brain is not made of stuff strong enough to contain forever the pressure of life or death uncertainty. I had to do something to relieve the pressure.

And, then, despite all our efforts and prayers to the contrary, I am watching Joey's downhill progress. He had so many hot spells today I lost count. He even agreed to let me make out his menu. "You want me to fill it out for you today, Joey?"

"Okay, mom," he said at last. "But read it out to me and I'll tell you what to circle. And for supper write in 'steak-rare' and 'yellow apple-peeled.'"

All I am doing is acknowledging the plot as I am watching it unfold.

Another Joey with C.F. is a patient in the ward across the hall. Most of the kids on the floor steer clear of our room, but this Joey knew our Joey from a previous hospitalization. A brave soul, he came to the door today and looked in. I felt as though a curse had been lifted.

"How's Joey doin', Mrs. Woodson?" he asked. And then his eyes lit on the shelf where we keep Joey's extra food. "Boy, he sure does have a lot of RCs."

RC is the only soft drink you can order from the cafeteria, and Joey has written in RC on both his lunch and supper menus every day since he's been here. Tonight as soon as he was asleep, I smuggled as many cans as I could under my coat and took them across the hall to the other Joey. He's a darling child, eight years old or so, with tousled blond curls and an accent echoing the West Virginia hills. His mother drives a taxi, and whenever a fare brings her close to the hospital she dashes in for a visit.

"Would you like to have some of Joey's RCs?" I asked. "Joey never will be able to drink all these."

And then I went off by myself and cried. I cried myself weak, but I felt strong, too. For it was true. Joey never would be able to drink all those RCs. Oh, God, it was true.

Late Third Monday Afternoon

Praying is not the only thing one needs a place to be alone for in the hospital—not if one has a husband anyway.

I walked with Joe to the elevator a few days ago. He pushed the up button and pulled me on the elevator with him. I knew what he had in mind. Oh, nothing illegal. Just a moment or two between floors when we would have the elevator to ourselves and could cling physically.

Before we could collect ourselves, however, the doors opened on the sixth floor—on the wildest scene I have ever witnessed. The foyer rocked with people, all waving their arms and screaming in mob hysteria.

"You pulled my baby!"

"I did not pull your baby!"

"She hit me!"

"Of course I hit him! I hit him 'cause he pulled my baby!"

"The only reason I pulled your baby—"

And then the whole fist-shaking multitude surged into our little elevator, flattening Joe and me against the back wall.

The doors closed, almost.

And then reopened. "Out!" commanded two hospital policemen.

We didn't know whether that included us or not, but Joe and I could not have moved if we had wanted to, for no one in that now-silent horde in front of us budged an inch.

"I said out!"

No one stirred.

"Are you comin' out or am I comin' in to get you?"

My goodness, they really do talk like that, I thought.

The smaller of the policemen collared the tallest of the men and hurled him into the hall. The many other tall men and the one unbelievably fat woman trotted docilely after him.

Innocent-eyed, Joe and I stayed glued to the back of the elevator. Our last glimpse of the sixth floor before the doors closed once more showed our erstwhile elevator mates, hands raised against the wall, being properly frisked.

"I'll never again push up when I'm supposed to be going down," Joe whispered, and we giggled all the way to the ground floor.

It was not a laughing matter, though, this whole thing of Joe's needing me. And a couple days later, which was yesterday, we had lunch together at a little Italian café a few blocks from the hospital, the only sidewalk café in our city. We couldn't afford that incomparable spaghetti and veal parmigiana, but we couldn't not afford it either. Joe held my hand under the red and white checkered tablecloth, and outdoor breezes blew away our preoccupation with everything but each other.

Joe said he wanted me to come home one day each week. That he needed me there in the house. That Peggie needed me in the house. That the house needed me. He said one of the nurses in the congregation would stay with Joey. I said it sounded good to me and I would come that very night.

But when we got back to the hospital, Joey greeted us with his usual, "What took ya so long?" And I could not leave him.

"He's too hot and weak today," I pleaded with Joe in the corner. "And he wants me."

Joe nodded understandingly.

"Tomorrow," I promised. "I'll definitely come tomorrow."

Which is today. But when Joe comes this morning . . .

Help me, Father. Help me remember Joe is the one constant

factor in my life, aside from You. When both the children are gone, he'll still be my base, and he needs me now more than he has ever needed me. Let me be fair to Joe.

And let Joe keep on understanding when I'm not.

Third Monday Night

A new intern came in tonight. "I'm taking over Joey's case," he said. The old intern, in the best tradition of interns, had moved on to another floor.

I felt badly that he didn't come in to say good-bye. He had taken care of Joey for quite a while now. Staggered out of bed in the middle of the night for one crisis or another. Always seemed to know the right thing to do and acted decisively.

I wasn't surprised, though, about his not saying good-bye. Joey usually seemed more of a case than a child to him. And never once had I been aware that he thought of Joey as my child.

What a contrast to the red-headed fellow I met one night at the grill. The cafeteria has a different air at night when the regular section is closed and just the grill is open. The few people who wander in talk to each other in a way the many who rush about in the daytime do not.

"It's been a long vigil for you, hasn't it?" the young man asked as we waited for our french fries. "How is Joey? It's hard just to watch and wait, isn't it?" He smiled at me, and it was not a bedside manner; it was tender loving care. I went back to my room and cried because somebody cared, therapeutic tears that washed away the lonely stain of what seemed a long vigil indeed.

And I didn't even know who the young man was, or what he was. Not a doctor. A medical student perhaps—half a doctor.

Well, he was on his way to being a whole doctor if his empathy continued to grow with his expertise.

He might even be as fine a doctor as Dr. Rathburn, unlikely as that seemed. How good it was to be confident that Dr. Rathburn knew all there was to be known about Joey's condition and that he was doing all there was to be done.

"Call me," he urges. "Anytime you're upset. There's no need for you to lie awake at night worrying when you can pick up the phone and call me."

I shouldn't be too hard on our old inhibited intern, though. I'm far from an extrovert myself. I have no right to put all the blame on the other fellow for the distance between us.

I shouldn't be too hard on the new interns either. Somebody told me that on the first of July hospitals all over the country do their basic switching about, old interns becoming new residents and old medical students becoming new interns. It's just that this batch looks so new as they walk in pairs down the hall, excited and peering about.

I know they have to learn on somebody, but does it have to be somebody as sick as Joey?

One of them walked into our room a short time ago with a lost expression in his eyes and a large needle in his hands. "Where do they usually take blood?" he quavered.

Thank You, Father, for all the people in this place who, in their mixture of power and pity, are a little bit like You. Let me absorb all they have to give and be glad for it.

And as far as the others are concerned, help me to be like You, loving those who are not able to love back and lifting up those who fall flat on their inexperienced faces.

Third Tuesday Morning

I looked up *hope* in my dictionary this morning—"a feeling that what is wanted will happen." Now I meant it when I said I had basically given up hope for Joey, but I also meant it when I said a part of me would hope on till the very end.

I wish it were not so. Hope is mean. It makes for too many moments of truth. Every time Joey takes a turn for the worse, I have to repeat the whole painful process of acceptance.

A minister friend came to visit this morning. "There are times," I told him, "when I think I could get through this more easily without God. If it were not for the possibilities inherent in a God both sovereign and solicitous, I would not be able to be let down the way I am being let down."

I wasn't nice to the minister. He represented God at the moment, and at the moment I was not feeling kindly toward God. "It would be better," I said, "if God never healed anybody. It's the way He picks and chooses that makes things hard."

"You mean to say you would rather live without hope?" the minister asked.

"Yes," I insisted. "If there is no hope for Joey, I would a thousand times rather live without hope."

I meant it when I said it, but I've wondered since if I really would favor that kind of bleakness. I think I would prefer any other ride to this out-of-control roller coaster I'm on, but I have never been on a ride that went on and on and on, on a perfectly level plane.

And even if I chose to live without hope for Joey, could I? I suspect that if I did not hope in God, I would find myself hoping in psychic surgery or wheat germ. I suspect hope springs eternal whether the human breast wishes it to or not.

I rarely deal with Peggie and Joey in just the same manner, though they resent the fact. Life would be more predictable for them if what I did for one I always did for the other. But they are different types, my two children, and their needs and circumstances vary greatly. How defeating to their best interests it would be if I always treated them alike.

Well, as long as we are the beloved children of God, He is going to treat us just that way, as individually loved children. And our hopes are going to be raised by what He does for another child and dashed when He does not do the same for us.

I must distinguish between certain and uncertain hopes. The hope that God will not let Joey die is an uncertain hope. The hope that I will avoid any particular tragedy of life is an inevitable hope, inevitable and irresolute. But the hope that God will work in a unique way in behalf of my unique personhood in whatever catastrophe comes my way—ah, that is a hope that will hold me steady however the gale blows.

Third Tuesday Noon

I went to church this noon urgently in need of the presence of God and utterly unable to find it. It's been like that a lot since Joey's been sick, but today it was especially like that.

I cried out my longing. Nothing.

I raised my voice in thanks and adoration. Nothing.

"Someone's crying, Lord," we sang. "Be with us." Yes, Lord, I pleaded. Please be with Joe and Peggie and Joey and me. We're crying so hard right now. Nothing.

Why don't you think of someone else who's crying? the Lord seemed to ask.

Am I not entitled even now to be consumed with my own need? I protested. But did as I was bidden.

That little girl two doors down from Joey who cries for her mama all day long, Lord, be with her. And that middle-aged man wandering around the hall today with a bewildered look in his eyes, he's crying on the inside, Lord. Be with him.

And I found, as I had found so many times in the past, that the Lord refreshes me best as He passes through me to meet the needs of others. Not that I try to lose my life just so I can find it. It is not a gimmick, but a law, for all times and under all circumstances.

Concentrating on the glory of God is first only to concentrating on the good of others. How can I be the much-loved daughter of my Father in heaven and ignore the rest of the family?

Exhaustion does make it hard to reach out, but isn't it my worried preoccupation with myself which leads to my exhaustion, which leads to further fear and depression, which leads to further exhaustion?

A cleaning woman shuffled in shortly after I got back to Joey, one of the parade of clean linen women and dirty linen women and sweepers and moppers and wastebasket emptiers who march in and out of this room with sunrise-sunset consistency. I had made a habit of trying not to talk to them, especially the garrulous types, which most of them were.

Well, this afternoon I struck up the conversation.

But when my inquiries about the cleaning woman's family had run their course, she took the initiative. "He your baby?" she asked, pointing to Joey.

"Yes, he's my baby." Strange she should put it that way when I'd reverted to calling Joey "baby" myself of late, a habit he would loudly disclaim had he the strength.

"I thought he was your baby. I was tellin' Mable yesterday, 'that mama in 414, she takes better care of her baby than any mama I ever done seen.'"

I gave her a chocolate bar, and she left happy, but not as happy as she left me. So, there was another reason for opening yourself up to people. For how could people get close enough to help you if you kept yourself all boarded up?

A little later as I was walking down the hall I came on Mrs. Chan pushing her daughter in a wheelchair. I had made a habit of avoiding this woman, too. Her poor English made communication difficult, and I could not bear the vacant stare on her daughter's large, round face.

"Hi, Mrs. Chan," I said now. "You've had a long vigil, haven't you? Your daughter—has been sick—a long time? It's hard just to watch and wait, isn't it?"

"It is two weeks," said Mrs. Chan, holding up two fingers, "two weeks she is confused in the head."

"I haven't been able to help noticing what good care you take of her," I said. "I'm sure you're the best nurse she has."

Mrs. Chan smiled a great, dazzling smile. "You think I am good nurse?" she asked. "Ah, nice."

It is true, of course, that all us sufferers must stand on our own feet. But how better can we manage this than by leaning heart-to-heart on our fellow travelers. I made my way back to room 414, but I belonged to a larger world. Ah, nice.

Third Tuesday Night

Visitors came tonight. Actually, friends have visited often since I've been keeping this diary. I don't know why I've said so little about them when their coming means so much. It's good to know the old, firm world is still intact. Familiar faces leave their special brand of strength behind.

Tonight's visitors talked to Joey more than they should have, though. He was so good about talking back that they had no way of knowing how it wore him out. But when they left he looked at me and panted in relief.

Joey is communicating more and more in sign language. A shake of the head or a shrug of the shoulders takes less out of him than spoken words. I marvel at the ever-growing rapport we establish sitting here in silence. I anticipate what Joey wants before he points. We are beyond needing to articulate our affection.

I was sitting beside Joey's bed tonight scribbling these observations in my notebook, when slowly all the flickers of light that have danced in and out of my mind for a couple weeks now concerning God's closeness to me converged in one blinding flash of love.

It wasn't just that God loved me as I loved my son—with the unspeakably joyous, unbearably anguished love with which I loved my son. God loved me as much as He loved His own Son.

It had to be. For hadn't He given His Son for me? It was not a blasphemy for me to overestimate God's love for me. It was not a possibility for me to overestimate God's love for me. God loved me with a perfect love.

Hadn't He been showing me right along that He identified with me—totally? That He understood me—wholly? That there was nothing He would not do for me, nothing He would not make of me? That it was His highest pleasure to be with me—forever?

His love was all one human being longed for from another elevated to some nth degree. There was a limit to the closeness I could achieve with Joey, in silence or in song. But there was a Person with whom the persistent human dream of perfect love really did come true.

God held nothing of Himself from me. He loved me not guardedly, not to a point. God loved me enough.

Late Third Tuesday Night

I thought I was done for the night. We still keep the room at arctic temperatures in an effort to keep Joey cool, and I snuggled down under the four hospital bedspreads I fold double on top of my cot in an effort to keep myself warm. But my insides, unaccustomed to encounters with absolute love, would be neither warm nor still.

I got up and prowled the halls. The hands on the big clock at the nurses' station pointed to two A.M. No matter. No way could I sleep. For it was not a head knowledge of God's love I wanted most basically. I did not want to be told I was loved as much as I wanted to be held tight in love.

Up and down and round and round the halls I went. "Are you all right, Mrs. Woodson?"the night nurse asked, giving me the anxious eye on my ninth stroll past the station.

"Yes, I'm fine," I told her. And I was, too. For as I wandered I couldn't help wondering about certain truths I had been taught even as a child.

About how God had dwelt among His people in unapproachable holiness in the Old Testament tabernacle, but how that had not been enough for God's love. And how He had then sent His Son to walk in human flesh right down here beside us, but how even that had not been enough for God's love. And how finally He had sent His Spirit to get right down inside us.

I could not remember a time when I had not known that we

created beings needed to become begotten beings, beings born of God's Spirit. Yet it flabbergasted me to think that God Himself was sharing His nature with me. Making me His son by making me of the same stuff as He.

How different the halls of a hospital are at night, hushed and dusklike. Nurses float about on the glow of their flashlights like white phantoms, and once-rambunctious boys and girls lie unnaturally still in sleep. Familiar shapes hide behind shadowy contours, and the least fancy of procedures become acts sublime.

I liked the transcendental air. It fitted my mood. I paced reverently up and down the empty corridors making peace with the mystery that rocked me. Odd how you experience God most intimately when you bow before His mystery.

God wanted to be near me. God could not get near enough to me. God wanted to be one with me.

God was one with me. Even as I padded the halls in my worn brown robe and fuzzy blue scuffs, the pleasure of His presence was so piercing as to be akin to pain. How filled with joy I was. How filled with peace. With strength. Love.

Has it not always been so for us sons of men when we recognize our destiny as sons of God? When we know finally that the love of God is the love above all others on which our desire is set, on which our need is bent?

Come home, the Father calls to every lonely one of us. Come home.

In relationship to Him we find our roots, the origin of our beings. In union with Him we find our nurture, our present well-being. In the heart of God we find our permanent dwelling place.

Third Wednesday Morning

Joey was moaning softly this morning. I jumped up from a nap and ran to him. "What's the matter, honey?"

"Nothing would be the matter if you'd leave me alone," he said nastily.

I went back behind my curtain and wept.

It wasn't only me he reacted to like this. The other day Nancy was doing everything she could to relieve his headache—bringing him an ice pack, raising his bed, adjusting his oxygen. "She's what gives me a headache," Joey snarled after she left.

I was the only one he snarled at face to face. And I tried so hard to meet his needs, and I valued every warm response from him so highly. I could never anticipate when he'd attack, and the unexpectedness of his dark spells unstrung me.

What made it hurt the most, though, was how unlike him it was to hurt me at all. I was a faultfinder by nature, and Joe brooded over insignificant slights, but Joey . . . "Oh, well," he'd say in response to some injustice, "that's the way the cookie rolls."

"*Crumbles*, dummy," Peggie would hoot. "That's the way the cookie *crumbles*."

Joey refused to be insulted.

I'm not saying he had never been provoked to anger, or even violence. Once a mother up the street called to inform me that her daughter had my son's teeth marks in her arm.

"Well," I responded indignantly, "I can't comment until I've talked to Joey." The woman was obviously confusing my son with some ordinary troublemaker.

And then it had been Joey. It seemed the girl had tormented him all the way home from school, pulling his jacket, threatening to throw his books in the creek. She was bigger than he and just wouldn't quit. Driven beyond his limits, Joey had sunk his teeth into her girlish flesh.

I would have to remember the extent to which pain and tiredness were provoking him now. It was continual exhaustion that drained him of control. Not me. It was never-ending pain he was attacking. Not me.

I'm making it sound as though all Joey does is fuss at me. Actually, his moments of ill-humor are so few they would not warrant mentioning were I not disproportionately vulnerable to them. Most of the time he is so uncharacteristically good, I cannot bear his goodness either.

Any effort he's asked to make depletes him; yet he cooperates with every effort asked. He even takes his pills without a protest, and for Joey that is the ultimate in goodness.

We had found his pills hidden all over the house for years— pink pills in the bottom of the sugar bowl, green pills under the living room rug. At school he stuffed all his pills in his milk container. The principal himself talked to Joey. We begged, reasoned, threatened, punished, rewarded.

During one of his hospitalizations they had to call the plumber to fix the heater in Joey's room. The plumber found the heater clogged with Joey's pills. That one got him sent to Peggie's old psychologist friend, Dr. Pearson.

"There's nothing wrong with him," Dr. Pearson reported. "Sure, he doesn't like having C.F., but he compensates with his intellectual pursuits."

I could have told them there was nothing wrong with Joey. He had made up his mind he was not going to take pills. His reasons were his own. End of discussion.

So when I saw him dutifully raise his head thirty or forty

times a day now and swallow his pills without a murmur, I thought my heart would break.

"How did you like Dr. Pearson?" I had asked during that other hospitalization.

"Well, he's okay. Only thing is he said we were going to tell each other stories, and I'm the only one who told any stories. The shrink fibbed," Joey had laughed. Somehow or other he'd come out on top in that encounter.

Usually he felt that way about himself. Contented and in control.

I've heard ministers say that salvation comes to us in three stages. We have been saved. We are in the process of being saved. And one day we will be saved ultimately. Well, death comes that way, too. When I look at this beloved son of mine, untypically disagreeable or untypically docile, I know I have lost him already. Know I am well into the process of losing him altogether.

Early Third Wednesday Afternoon

Joey had to make a second trip to the bathroom just now. I can take it once a day, but twice does me in. Partly because I can't help remembering how his trips to the bathroom used to be.

I could never miss the precise moment Joey got home from school—the crashing in of the front door, the thudding of his books on the floor, the wild galloping of his feet as he charged the downstairs bath. Engrossed in a variety of enticing activities, he never could be bothered with the necessities of life till the last desperate moment.

Now his life consists of nothing but physical necessities, and how laboriously he executes them.

His trips to the bathroom are still the only times I get to hold him. "It feels so good to hold you, Joey," I tell him. And it does feel good.

But it feels bad, too. Oh, how bad it feels to be hugging so much feebleness and so little bulk. Most of the time his pajamas conceal how little is left of him, but when he's in the bathroom he can't manage for himself, and I have to pull down his pajamas. . . .

Who is this child with the grossly distended stomach standing on skeleton legs in Joey's bathroom?

What's all this talk I hear about death with dignity? About death being a natural process and our not doing anything to destroy the peace and beauty of the natural process? Death is an ugly, unnatural process. God never created man to have body and soul rent apart. What death accomplishes for us may be accomplishment indeed, but its procedure is an affront.

I am glad, Father, that You call death our enemy, the final enemy that has not yet been destroyed. Thank You for preparing a place for us where it will be again as it was in the beginning. Thank You for preparing an end to the obscene end.

Middle of Third Wednesday Afternoon

Joe always has devotions with Joey when he comes to the hospital. Today he read one of the descriptions of heaven in the Book of Revelation.[11] "These are they who have come out of the great tribulation," he began.

"What's the tribulation?" Joey interrupted, in sharp departure from a life-long disinterest in anything resembling the tribulation.

"Well," Joe replied, in loosest of interpretations, "those who come through the great tribulation are those who come through a lot of suffering. And one thing the Bible says about these people is that in heaven they never get tired. How about that?" he asked Joey meaningfully. "See, it says it right here:

> Therefore are they before the throne of God,
> and *serve him day and night* within his temple;
> and he who sits upon the throne will shelter them
> with his presence."

"What about getting hot?" I asked. "Does the Bible say anything about people not having hot spells in heaven?" I gave Joey a conspiratorial nod. This time we had Joe stumped.

"Well, yes, it does," Joe answered smugly. "Right here in the next verse as a matter of fact:

> They shall hunger no more, neither thirst any more;
> the sun shall not strike them, *nor any scorching heat.*"

Joey rolled his eyes upward, and Joe read the last verse:

> For the Lamb in the midst of the throne will be their
>   shepherd,
>   and he will guide them to springs of living water;
>   and God will wipe away *every tear* from their eyes.

Mmmm, I thought. I suppose if you used enough sanctified imagination, you could find a verse in the Bible to promise that whatever load weighed you down in this life would be lifted in the next. Well, why not? It was true, wasn't it, whether or not one's specific limitation was mentioned? *Every tear* was a fairly inclusive phrase.

Later Third Wednesday Afternoon

Joe and I went down to the Parents' Lounge this afternoon and talked about Joey's funeral. Oh, our conversation was full of ifs, but that is what we talked about.

It seemed important to both of us that Joey's funeral be held in our church, a place of worship, for a service of worship we determined it would be. The only thing on which we disagreed was whether the opening hymn should be "All Hail the Power of Jesus' Name" or "Joyful, Joyful, We Adore Thee." I finally told Joe he could plan the whole rest of the service if he would let me have "Joyful, joyful, we adore Thee. . . . Hearts unfold like flowers before Thee."

I talked about my dream that this diary I'm working on might become a book someday to help other people going through what we were going through. And Joe talked about his overseas orphan idea. "If we could find a child who doesn't have a home and take him into our home, it would be something we'd do as a result of Joey's death that we would not otherwise do," he explained. "A way of continuing Joey's influence."

"I never told you this before, Joe," I confided, "but quite a while ago when I was praying one day I told the Lord it would be all right with me if our children died if through their deaths a cure could be found for all C.F. children. I don't know how it could happen . . . but wouldn't it be the most wonderful thing?"

Joe gave me his handkerchief then so I could wipe my eyes.

What a wonderful thing it would be indeed if our child could be a child on God's own mission, not only in death, but after death, in heaven but also on this earth God and Joey loved so well.

Third Thursday Morning

The doctor who heads the C.F. Center made rounds this morning.

"When am I gonna get out of here?" mumbled Joey, glad for a new authority to whom to pose the old question.

"What's that, Joey?"

"When am I gonna—ya know—go home?"

"Your going home is what we're all working for, Joey," the doctor replied.

Nice, I thought. Nice answer. But not true. Not for the doctors, nor for me. Not any more.

I know there are a number of stages people often go through when they face death, for themselves or others. When all this is over, I'll look them up. See if I'm normal with my movement from acceptance of whatever the will of God might be, to acceptance of death as His will, to active consent to that death.

One thing I'm sure is normal is the backward-forward movement obvious in these scribblings. I can't help seeing overall forward movement, though. Nor can I imagine anything beyond this ready agreeing with God's will I'm doing now.

I was standing beside Joey's bed this morning before he was awake, looking down at him.

I love you, Joey. I say it a lot these days.

Other people had three or four sons. Other people had sons

who were nothing but trouble. But I had just one son, and what a prize.

But then it occurred to me that if I truly loved Joey, I should be glad he was going. That who I was loving was me—me first and Joey second. That while I had accepted death for Joey as God's ruling, I had not accepted it as my own. And right then I assented to what was best for Joey.

For his life to go on as it was would be unendurable for him. If he was not going to get well, I had to turn loose of him, give my blessing to his exit from the frail frenzy of this life and his entrance into the freedom of the next.

Even while he lived he would profit, would he not, from the release of tension within me? Must he not feel guilty about the sorrow he was causing me?

Let Joey come to You soon, Father. I've just had a glimpse of Your love, Your hand on my head now and then. Let Joey enter fully into Your life, Father.

Though I could not stop Joey's death if I chose, I could by my approval achieve the virtue and value of a voluntary sacrifice.

Third Thursday Afternoon

It took me a while to realize it was a holiday today—the Fourth of July.

Peg and Joe came over around noon. "On Memorial Day I took Joey down to the roof on the second floor for a picnic lunch," Joe reminisced. "A band entertained. Joey walked to the elevator and out on the roof."

Joey said he wanted to go down in his wheelchair today. Or perhaps we said he wanted to. At any rate, when the time came he backed out. "I'm too tired," he cried. It was just as well. Acrobats were performing on the roof today. How would Joey have felt, slumped in his wheelchair, watching those lithe bodies swirling through the air?

I've been trying to record only events of wider significance in this diary. Well, something happened to that effort today. Joey ate his Fourth of July chicken in his hospital bed. It happened. It was significant.

Peggie took our gloom for just so long before she exploded. "Is this a holiday or is this not a holiday? What you need around here is a roommate, Joey. A roommate like me. Remember how I cheered Jenny up when she was in for so long?"

Jenny was one of Peggie's best C.F. friends, their hospitalizations often coinciding.

"Remember how she had that tube in her chest that time and they were supposed to keep changing the dressing and they never did and I glued the scissors and bandages and ointment and all to the dressing tray and nobody even knew for the longest time?

"That's what we need around here—stuff like that.

"And remember that night I laid in wait under the covers with Jenny's flashlight when it was time for our two o'clock medications and it was all dark and when Nancy walked in I turned on the flashlight and jumped out and yelled 'Boo'?"

"What did Nancy say to that?" asked Joe.

"Well, she almost dropped the meds," giggled Peg. "And what she said is not appropriate for your ears, father.

"And the first time I was in with Jenny? That was the funniest time of all. Remember how she left with her parents right after she checked in and I hadn't even met her yet and the nurse said they were going to the cafeteria and I could eat her chicken? So I took the chicken off her plate and put the cover back on and ate the chicken and then Jenny came back and sat down to eat.

"And I was yellin', 'The nurse told me I could eat it. Hello, I'm your roommate, Peggie. The nurse told me I could eat it.'"

Holidays had always been special times of togetherness for our family. Well, even though Peggie did most of the talking and Joey none, we were all together. Even laughing together. We made it through the Fourth of July.

It happened. It was significant.

Third Thursday Night

One of the first things we said to the doctor when we brought Joey back to the hospital this time was, "We want to be with him if he dies. We don't want him to die alone."

"I know all about that," Dr. Rathburn had replied, and we realized our desire must be the universal desire of parents of dying children.

Later we learned that having their parents with them is the universal desire of dying children as well. There are two things they want, Edie told us. First, to know that everything that can be done for them is being done, and, second, that they will not be alone when death comes.

Death doesn't always arrive on schedule, though, allowing appropriate intervals for proper farewells. At times God may honor our requests as far as the details are concerned, but usually He appears to leave us subject to the normal death process as it moves on its sometimes slow, sometimes sudden, frequently whimsical way.

So I must prepare myself. I do on occasion have to step out of the room. If it happens that I am not with Joey when he dies, my biggest comfort will stem from already having said the things I want him to know before he goes, about how much I love him and about the new world he's bound for. What is more important—that I be with Joey in that future, final moment, or that I be a good mother to him now in every sacred-present moment?

I will be with you, Joey, if I possibly can. Though I have the idea that when death arrives it will be the friend you seek, not I. Yet you know I will be with you if I can. But in case it doesn't work out, please, Joey, hear the good-byes I'm whispering to you now in all of my hellos.

Fourth Friday Afternoon

Everyone has some addiction. It is my misfortune to be addicted to food, and never more of a misfortune than right now.

Joey always leaves something on his tray. Huge bunches of seedless grapes, for example, the kind we can rarely afford at home. It would be a sin to throw them away, would it not?

What exciting event breaks the monotony of these bleached, starched days if not the coming of meal trays? Where is there to go when the monotony of these staring-into-space days dictates that I must go someplace other than to the cafeteria?

I eat so effortlessly. It demands none of my dwindling energy supply.

And I do feel better when I overeat. I'm frightened here. I feel rejected by Joey's dying. What better way to fill the void within than by stuffing myself physically?

The problem, of course, is that the relief I experience is temporary. Given a little time gluttony adds weight not only to my derriere but to my self-doubt as well. I lose my self-love— and my awareness of the love of God.

Oh, but God understands, I argue. He'll overlook a slip at a time like this. Can I think God is looking down from His terrible heights gloating over my failure? Aha! Meg Woodson ate two large pieces of chocolate fudge cake. I'll take Joey's life.

Is God some cosmic sadist or is He my Father?

Well, of course, He's my Father. And, of course, He's not going to punish me with Joey's death for two large pieces of chocolate fudge cake.

Though Satan is going to capitalize on my weakness, I'm afraid. He is no gentleman, leaving me alone while I'm having so hard a time. He's a devil pure and simple. "She's having it rough, boys," he cackles. "After her!"

And the Lord our God is still one Lord. It's not so much that He won't draw me close if I overeat as that He can't, at least not as close as He could if I worshiped Him alone. For overeating is no minor indulgence for me. I'm not your average nibbler, your ten-or-twenty-pound overweighter. My endless gorging of myself is a god to which I look for the gratification for which I should be looking only to the true God.

How can the true God meet my needs if I insist they be met by green grapes?

Overeating diminishes me, as surely as drinking diminishes the alcoholic, or lusting diminishes the adulterer, or putting somebody else down diminishes the gossip.

How easy to let self-pity take over. Poor thing, I tell myself. You should have an RC for what you're going through. It's not good for you or Joey when you're this tense. Remember how a little snack always relaxes you?

But poor thing I am indeed if I forfeit the fullest presence of God for an RC.

Fourth Friday Night

Joey is drawing further within himself, withdrawing further from us.

His carbon dioxide continues to inch its way up; his fatigue increases. He lies on the bed in a new kind of dense, excluding silence, broken only by his sobbing when the periods of heat plummet down on him and the pain in his head rockets.

Joe and I have been living with such heightened awareness of what's going on inside us that it's hard not knowing what's going on inside Joey. "What are you thinking these days, son?" Joe asked him recently.

Joey rolled over. Gave us his back. "I'm tired. I just wanna be left alone," he whimpered. And though we knew it was a physical thing, it hurt that what he did more than anything else these days was roll away from us.

In the old days I'd been free to coax Joey into expressing his feelings. "Joey doesn't love me. Oh, boo hoo," I'd cry.

"Come on, mom," he'd say in exasperation. "I love ya. Ya know I love ya." And he would plop in my lap, scootching his bony rump back and forth in an effort to seal our relationship.

No more.

"I sure am glad I have you for a son," Joe said to him yesterday, waiting expectantly for Joey to reply.

Joey said nothing.

Please, God, let him say something to his father, something his father can hold fast to through the years.

And finally Joey had spoken. "I'm glad I'm your son, too," he mumbled.

How pleased Joe was.

But then Joey added one of his typical Joey afterthoughts. "Of course, if I wasn't your son, I don't know whose son I'd be."

Joe had laughed, but there were tears in his voice as he responded. "Oh, Joey, don't say that. You're glad you're my son, right?"

Joey had nodded.

If he weren't able to think, his retreat would be easier to take. But he could think. A comment like "If I wasn't your son, I don't know whose son I'd be" was the product of a mind in good working order. And he could talk when he wanted to. He made an effort to talk to everybody else.

My hurt became more than I could contain tonight when I stooped and pressed my lips in that special kissing spot in Joey's neck. He had never failed once through all these weeks to respond when I did this, and tonight was no exception, his shoulder coming up and cradling my face. But then as I stood looking down at him I realized his shoulder coming up like that was the result of his laborious breathing. It came up like that every second or so whether I kissed him or not.

I didn't even have that.

I ran from the room and down the hall, locking myself in the Parents' Lounge and crying as I had not cried since we brought Joey back to the hospital.

But then I got thinking about a spell of airsickness I'd had the summer before when our family had flown over New York City in a small sightseeing plane. I had laid back in my seat unmoving, unwilling even to turn my head. "Leave me alone. Don't talk to me," I gasped.

As the plane bounced on and on, I actually wanted to die. Don't you care anything about your family? I upbraided myself.

Not at all, I responded.

"She doesn't want to be bothered," I heard Peggie whisper to Joey. "Don't even touch her."

I heard the hurt in her voice, but I cared about nothing but the sweating and the nausea.

The passenger behind me offered me a motion-sickness pill. I turned and smiled at him. "No, thank you," I said politely. "I've already taken two."

But to have acted politely with my family would have been impossible. Anyway, my relationship with my family would survive despite my unpleasantness. My unpleasantness was a tribute to the security of that relationship.

Could I think it was different with Joey? Hadn't I been proud when he had willed his books to Peggie and his money to the roof fund without one last look? Well, wasn't I one of his possessions? Didn't he have to give me up, too?

He might not often let us know what was going on inside him, but we knew something good was going on.

"How are you today, Joey?" Joe asked several visits ago.

"Oh, pretty good," Joey replied. "Ya know God says He never puts more on ya than ya can stand."

We couldn't believe those spiritually mature words were coming out of our Joey. He was pushing us behind him, but he was reaching out to the One who waited just ahead.

And he did miss me when I left him. Didn't he always protest my absence when I got back? I felt chastened by his accusing "Where were ya?" But I felt comforted, too.

All of which reminded me that I had been gone too long right then, and I hurried back to the room. I waited for Joey's "What took ya so long?" But he said nothing. I waited for a simple "I wanted ya." But I got nothing.

He was awake. He was alert. But he'd missed me not at all.

A month has passed. Or is it two? I am disoriented where time is concerned. When it is dark around the clock, it is hard to tell when one day ends and another begins.

Part of me knows it is daytime now. They only open the gates here in the daytime. Just as part of me knows this is a green place, an almost-nothing-but-green place.

But the freshly turned mound of dirt beside which I stand is not green, the swollen stomach of brown earth that has swallowed my son. Nothing identifies the spot. I wandered about wretchedly trying to find it.

I see in my mind the marker we have ordered. "Joseph Woodson Jr." it says, with the dates of Joseph Woodson Jr.'s birth and death below. A small cross imposed upon a shepherd's crook is under the dates. Joe insisted on that, and on the words on the bottom of the marker: "With Christ — Far Better."

"We want 'Beloved Son' in there someplace," I said.

"And Brother!" Peggie added.

"Do we need that?" Joe asked, shy at public endearments.

"We need that," I maintained.

We need that, I maintain. All of us who have prayed that we be spared a horror and have not been spared. We need to look the horror in the face, six feet under and artificially rouged though it be. We must not hide from the horror. But neither must we let the horror hide the comfort that marks the spot where it lies.

We have that comfort, I maintain. All crumbled brown mounds that cover human disintegration of whatever sort are so marked. I have that comfort.

I walk from the grave to a tree a few yards away. It is green, the tree. I sit on the grass. It, too, is green. Suddenly all of me knows this is an altogether-nothing-but-new-life place.

I take my spiral notebook from my purse. I must finish the record. It will be hard, and yet not hard. For they are not in the past, those last days. They will be forever present in my mind and heart, those last days, that

Last Saturday

Grandfather brings Joe over early in the morning. "I think you should go home today," Joe says. "I'll stay with Joey."

I am stunned. He is not asking me if I want to go. I do not understand. I thought he wanted me at home to be with him. I look at Joey and tears well in my eyes.

"Joey will be fine," Joe says. "Meg, go home."

I have to admit that Joey seems better. I ask Dr. Rathburn if he thinks anything will happen to Joey today. He does not think so.

I do not want to go, but at length I am persuaded. "Just for an hour or two," I insist.

* * * * *

I cannot believe how good it is to be home. My mother and father are doing a fine job with the house, but it is too big for them to keep dust-free the way Peggie needs it. I dash about shaking out rugs and mopping the kitchen floor.

"For goodness sakes, will you stop working?" my parents scold. "Rest while you have the chance." I am so used to taking care of someone else, I cannot believe how good it is to have someone else taking care of me. I try on the new blouses mother has bought me.

Peg and I talk. I did not realize how much I had missed her. How unfair I have been never getting away from Joey to be with her. Going down to the hospital cafeteria is not getting away from Joey. But coming home is, to a surprising degree.

"I'm havin' trouble with my new bike, braking with my hands," Peg says. "But I think I'll get it." She drags me out to the garage to inspect the bike. "Do you like it, mama? Do you really like it?

"Mrs. Williams took me out to lunch the other day," she confides. "We went to Mac's Place. She asked me if I liked Mac's Place, and I said I did." She eyes me guiltily.

I hug her and cry.

I am a keeper of a house, a daughter, a mother of a not-in-the-hospital child. I am renewed.

Now it is my turn to feel guilty. By the time we make the trip across town Joey will have finished supper.

* * * * *

I race through the lobby. Never have the elevators been as slow as they are today. My heart thuds with my feet as I race down the fourth floor corridor.

They are still there. Joe is sitting beside Joey with a radiance about him.

"How are you, Joey?"

"Oh, pretty good."

"It's been wonderful to have a whole day with Joey," Joe tells me. "I made out his menu and I cut his steak. I carried him to the bathroom. He said he wanted raisins, and I went out and got him some. Remember how he's always loved raisins?

"I even worked on the Tarzan model a little. Joey didn't feel like doing anything, but I sat beside him and worked on it. Sometimes I just sat beside him."

"I'm glad you had a chance to be with him," I say. How selfish I have been in my selfless devotion to Joey. No wonder Joe pushes me out of the room every time he comes to the hospital. When we are all together, Joey naturally turns to me with his physical needs, the only needs he has.

How shut out fathers must feel just when they need to be in.

* * * * *

Joey's legs feel funny. He wakes me in the night crying with the funny feeling in his legs. "No, they don't hurt, but they're so restless. Will you rub them for me, mama?"

I rub his legs. How precious they are, these restless sticks of bone of my bone. "Why do my legs have this funny feeling?" he quavers.

It does bring him out of his grogginess, though. Temporarily it lifts the foggy shroud that hides him from me. What a change in him at midnight compared to early this morning. He is truly groggy tonight.

I would not have left you, Joey, if I had known it was going to be like this. Oh, Joey, I would not have left you.

It is midnight, and I think it is the beginning of the end. I am not prepared. He was doing so well today, but he is groggy now and his legs feel funny. I am up and down for the rest of the night rubbing Joey's legs.

Rubbing and remembering dreams that have plagued me for as long as I can remember. Peggie and Joey are prisoners in a Nazi concentration camp. I rescue them. Peggie and Joey are stranded in a blizzard in the high Rockies. I rescue them.

I always lead the children to sanctuary, whether to a cave deep in some alien valley or to an abandoned shack on an American mountainside. I hold tightly to their hands, never letting them get lost or taken from me.

I chop firewood to keep them warm. I devise games to keep them occupied. I provide pure water and high-protein food. And always, miraculously, in some cobwebby corner I find the enzymes and the precise antibiotics they need at the moment. Always and under impossible circumstances I keep my children alive.

Yet I am right to say I am plagued by these dreams, for they foreshadow a time when I will not be able to save my children. This present time. This, for a parent, worst of all helpless times.

I know, God, that Your Fatherhood includes the compulsion to save Your children, to keep us fully alive, close by Your side forever. And I suspect that this present age when even You must watch helplessly as we dangle in our ever-dying despair must be the worst of all ages for You.

For You gave up some of Your power when You created us

with power of our own, did You not, Father? When You embarked on Your grand love-Me-if-you-will experiment? And, being God, You cannot go back on the choice You gave us. Nor can You with a wave of Your hand undo the consequences of our choice.

Nor would You go back on Your word if You could. For no way can we love You but by our option, and I suspect You find our love worth the suffering, Yours and ours. Am I really worth that much to you, Father?

"It's okay, Joey. Mother's here. See if you can sleep, Joey."

Would I have brought Joey into the world, I wonder, if I had known that loving him would result in this hell? I do not wonder long. It has been more than worth it all, the love of Joey.

I did not always find the love of God worth human suffering. I used to say that was the first question I would ask when I saw Him. If You knew that as a result one mother would sit by the bedside of one dying son, why didn't You stop the whole mad experiment before You started it?

But I did not know God's love then as I know it now.

And when I stand before Him, when I stand before Love, then I will know truly that the love of God is infinitely more than worth it all. That God's willingness to let me suffer is not evidence against His love but for it.

Last Sunday

"I'm cold, mama. Turn up the heat."

Oh, God, he's cold. Joey says he's cold.

I push up the thermostat. I button his pajama tops and cover him with sheets and blankets. I take off my coat. I reach under the covers and rub his legs. It seems like hours that I sit and rub his legs.

He is groggy and his legs feel funny and he is cold. I cannot think about it.

Joe drives to the hospital right from church. "Why is it so hot in here?" he asks.

"Hot?" wails Joey. "Why is it so cold?"

Joe moves casually into the hall.

"Joey is cold," I tell him. "And his legs have this funny feeling. He wants them rubbed all the time. And he's really groggy, Joe. He keeps having spells when I can hardly reach him."

Joe walks back into the room, picking up a planter with a statue of Christ on the front holding a little lamb. "Jesus is your Shepherd, Joey," Joe says. "A good shepherd knows every sheep by name. Did you know that Jesus is calling you by name?"

Joe sits beside the bed and rubs Joey's legs. I cannot look at the love with which Joe looks at his son.

* * * * *

Aunt Connie calls from Texas. "She wants to know if you'd like her to send you a book, Joey."

"Yeah. A Hardy Boy book. I still don't have numbers nine, twenty-two, or thirty-one."

Oh, Joey.

How can he be so groggy one minute and so alert the next?

Our minister friend comes to visit. Joe wants us to have communion together. The tiny therapist is working on Joey and we ask her to join us. We use grape juice in small medicine vials and low-sodium bread.

"This bread stands for the body of Christ, Joey," says the minister. "When you eat it, you are accepting the forgiveness of your sins for which Christ gave His body."

Joey nods and eats the bread. It is his first communion.

"This juice stands for the blood of Christ," says Joe. "Your Good Shepherd loved you so much He gave His life for you."

Joey drains the cup. Never does he say "I just wanna be left alone" when his father talks to him of God.

"Remember when Dave was here the other night?" Joe asks me in the corner. "Well, Dave's an elder, you know, and he and I asked Joey the questions the elders would have asked him at the end of the year when he joined the church. I didn't say anything to Joey, but I reported it to the elders, and they agreed, should Joey die, that they would accept his answers as his profession of faith."

I nod appreciatively. How moved Joe is by his son's formal confession.

We have not seen Dr. Rathburn all day. This is the first day since Joey has been in that we have not seen him. It makes me appreciate how available he has been. We could call him, but he deserves a day off, and I am sure there is nothing he can do.

We cannot find our intern either. Finally we find another intern. "Joey's groggy. Would you do a blood gas on him?"

The intern comes back, face beaming. "Joey's much improved," he reports.

"How can that be?" We explain how Joey's been acting.

"I don't know," says the young man, "but his carbon dioxide is definitely down."

Joe and I look at each other in perplexity. We do not want any more ups and downs.

Joe puts his hand on Joey's chest. "I love you, son," he says. "You're everything as a person I could possibly want." Joe is no more convinced by the intern's words than I.

Last Monday

An attendant comes up early to take Joey to x-ray.

"Wait here for a minute," I tell him.

I find the doctor. "Joey is too tired. He can't make it down to x-ray." For me it is a big rebellion.

"If he can't, he can't," Dr. Rathburn replies.

"The doctor says you don't have to go, Joey."

"I wish somebody'd make up their minds around here," the attendant grumbles.

But Joey's look of gratitude more than compensates. I should have rebelled a long time ago.

Joe comes over early and we take turns rubbing Joey's legs.

An attendant arrives with portable x-ray equipment. It is the big event of the morning.

"I like my new glasses," Joe says, apropos of nothing.

"I like your new glasses, too," Joey says.

Joe runs into the hall and cries. "I never knew I could cry this much," he tells me. "I pray it will be over soon. Either way. That it will just be over soon."

* * * * *

Joey uses the bedpan after lunch. This is the big event of the afternoon. He has staunchly refused the bedpan all these weeks. I support him now as he sits up in bed on the shiny, metal pan. It is more than a pan. It is a white flag waved by a valiant warrior who has fought himself out.

* * * * *

Joey sleeps on and off. Each time he goes to sleep I have to keep myself from shaking him awake. Mostly he lies there halfway between waking and sleeping.

He rouses himself for supper. He cannot be dying. No child who eats three waffles for breakfast and a whole steak for supper can be dying.

Friends come to visit. Joe leaves to meet some commitment. I walk the friends to the elevator.

When I return to the room, Joey is gasping for breath. "I can't—get enough—air—in my lungs—I want—my old—mask back."

Dr. Rathburn is waiting for me in the hall. "Joey is in imminent danger. His carbon dioxide's gone sky-high."

"But how can that be? Last night the intern said—"

"Something obviously went wrong with the test last night. Joey's count is ninety-eight. The machine only goes to a hundred. I've given him a mask with a smaller oxygen capacity."

"He says he wants his old mask back."

"I'll raise his oxygen."

"No! Remember you said you'd only do that when all hope was gone?"

"Let me make the decision."

"What will happen exactly?" I have to hear it again.

"He'll go to sleep. He just won't wake up."

I run to the phone and locate Joe. "Joey's in imminent danger. Come quickly, Joe."

I fly back to the room.

"Air! Air!" gasps Joey.

Joey's camp director comes down from Inhalation Therapy with a larger mask. "That better now, Joey?" he asks gently.

In a few minutes Joey is breathing easily. "Good, good," he says. "My old mask."

I bend over his bed. "The doctor says you may not be with us much longer, Joey." It seems right that he should know.

"What do you mean?"

"He thinks you're going to be with Jesus very soon now."

Silence.

"How do you feel about that?"

"I'd like that. I just wanna be done with all this."

"I surely will miss you, Joey. No other boy in the whole world could have brought me as much happiness as you."

Silence.

Silence.

He just wants to be done with all this.

* * * * *

Joe bursts into the room. We hug each other. We cry. Grandmother and grandfather come in with Peggie. We hold hands and pray.

I put my arm around Peggie and tell her that Joey is going to die very soon.

Joe goes down the hall to call his parents. He cannot remember how to dial long-distance. He asks the operator to help. He asks her to repeat the process.

"Well, now, let's see if you can get it this time," she says sarcastically.

Joe explodes. "My son is dying, operator. Help me."

* * * * *

Joey is sleeping. It seems a normal sleep.

Joe puts his hand on Joey's chest. "God be with you till we meet again, son." Joe locks himself in the waiting room a few doors down the hall and lies on the couch.

Joey calls for the urinal, but he cannot wait. He wets himself a little. He is embarrassed beyond reckoning. A great twelve-year-old boy wetting his pants. I change his clothes and his bed by myself. "Everybody has an accident once in a while," I tell him. "Nobody has to know but us."

A little later the whole process repeats itself. But this time Joey is only half aware of what is happening. This time Joey is not embarrassed.

I black out for a moment. I am covered with sweat. My stomach churns. Joey is not the only one who cannot make it to the bathroom.

Last Tuesday

5:00 A.M. Joey is soaking wet. He is not aware of it at all. The nurse helps me change him.

"I'm cold, mama."

I sit beside him and rub his legs.

"I'm starved."

I peel him a banana.

"I changed my mind," he mumbles.

"That's okay, Joey. Your waffles will be here after a while. Save your appetite for your waffles."

7:30 A.M. Joe picks up the Good Shepherd planter. "You're this little lamb, Joey. Safe in Jesus' arms. You don't have to do anything to have the hospital bed hold you up, do you? Well, it's the same way with Jesus. He's holding on to you.

"Do you understand, son? Nod your head if you understand."

Joey nods.

A therapist comes in to work on Joey. I motion her into the hall. "No more therapy. I won't have him put through it."

"You'll have to check with the doctor about that."

"I can't stop the routine," Dr. Rathburn tells me. "If I change the routine, the child realizes he's dying and panics."

"But Joey already knows he's dying, and he's not afraid."

The doctor thinks this over. "I never had a patient who had

no fear of death before. Ask Joey if he wants therapy. If he says no, it's no."

Joey says no. Never in his life, given a chance, did Joey not say no to therapy.

8:15 A.M. Breakfast arrives. "Your waffles are here," I say brightly.

Joey does not respond.

"Lie down, Meg," Joe urges. "There's no point in our both being awake at the same time. Joey may need you tonight."

I pull the curtain and lie on my cot.

Peggie calls. "I sure am glad you told me right out last night about Joey. What if he died and I didn't know he was goin' to? You should tell a person right out. And not 'Joey is going to pass away.' That's dumb. I mean, I know you say you told me, but I never heard you tell me."

"Do you remember when your Sunday school teacher was here?" I hear Joe asking Joey. "And he wanted to know if you had Jesus in your heart, and you said you did? Well, we took that as your profession of faith, and the officers received you as a member of the church.

"Do you want that to be your profession of faith, Joey?"
Silence.

"Squeeze my finger if you want that to be your profession."
Later Joe tells me of the pressure on his finger and of the emphatic nodding of Joey's head.

I resume my watch.

10:15 A.M. I cannot wake Joey up to take his pills. "I can't wake him up, Joe."

The nurse shakes him, slaps him. "Leave the pills here for a while," she says.

Joe and I sit in silence, our eyes riveted on Joey. Later Joe tells me of the coldness in Joey's hands and feet, a creeping coldness.

Where are You, God? I thought You would be so near, and I cannot feel Your presence at all.

Don't you remember, My own dear daughter? I'm right here with My arms around you. I sure am glad you belong to Me, Meg. I sure do love you.

I had no heavenly visitation. I dredged the voice from my own groggy consciousness.

And Joey? You love him, too, right? And Joe and Peg? And every last member of Your cursed human race? Your cursed, beloved human race?

Suddenly Joey's body goes into a sort of rag-doll heaving. "Joe! Joe! He's going. Now."

Joe puts his arm around me trying to cover my eyes, but I insist on looking. I wanted so badly to be here, and be here I will.

Some people see a light at such times, I am told. Some feel a Compassion. Some children cry out in delight or smile wondrous smiles.

But it is hardly a child I watch. It is a machine with several defective parts grinding slowly and suddenly to a halt. Coils spring. Water spouts. The machine smokes. The machine stops.

Yet it is not a machine I watch. It is a boy. My Joseph Woodson, Jr. boy, and he is dead. Oh, God.

Tuesday. July 9. 11:45 A.M.

The nurses rush in.

"Just a minute," Joe says, and places his hand once more on Joey's chest—on Joey's still, flat chest. "I am the resurrection and the life," Joe quotes our Lord. "He that believeth in me, though he were dead, yet shall he live. And whosoever liveth and believeth in me shall never die."

"Will you folks please step outside?" asks the resident.

I do as I am told. But first I take one last look at the bed and what is left of my beloved son—beloved son—beloved son. And my heart is not tomb cold as it would be were it not for those words. For he is home, my Joey. Where every love-hungry human heart longs to be.

Is he wandering about patting things contentedly? Being fussed over, welcomed by his heavenly family as Joe and Peg and I welcomed him home three short weeks ago?

Yeah, yeah! I hear him say. Joey is home all right.

And I am home, too. I walk from the room. It is a place of death I leave. But it is also a place of love. It is an altogether-nothing-but-new-love place.

Footnotes

1. Luke 3:22
2. Psalm 121:4
3. Romans 8:31-32
4. Ephesians 1:4-5
5. Romans 8:38-39
6. Romans 8:15-17
7. Romans 8:29; John 1:14, 16-17
8. Colossians 1:16; Hebrews 1:2
9. John 10:10
10. 2 Peter 1:16-19
11. Revelation 7:13-17

Contributions for Cystic Fibrosis research may be sent to:

The Joey Woodson Memorial Fund
Cystic Fibrosis Foundation
3091 Mayfield Road, Suite 310
Cleveland Heights, Ohio 44118